# Simply Be at 33

# Simply Be at 33

## Andrea Polakova

Published by A. Polakova


© Copyright Andrea Polakova 2019


SIMPLY BE AT 33

ISBN 978-1-5272-3493-2

Book formatted by www.bookformatting.co.uk.
Copy-editing : www.richardmsheehan.co.uk
Book cover design: www.bookbeaver.co.uk

# Contents

# Dedication

I dedicate this story to human beings from all walks of life that crossed my path and touched my soul in one way or another, to all beautiful fairies out there and dark witches too, to the awakened soul as well as to a lost one, to an ordinary man and a woman, to a child and to an elderly person and to the highs and lows of one's life.

Because the light will not exist without the darkness, and that same light would not be there if you didn't pass through the dark tunnel first, because without a woman there would not be a man and without them no child that would grow old and wise. I surrender my soul to the power of nature, which I worship most of all.

And in the natural contrast of all existence, I bring the experience of my truth – the story of my life to you…

# 1. Beacon of Light

A fairy tale would start with 'Once upon a time', but this isn't a story that's made up. This is the first part of a journey of a life. As such, I will not start my story from the early beginnings, because there was one event that allowed me to look at the world from a brand new perspective, allowed me to see a new light emerging.

In September 2005 I finally broke the cycle of me continually being an au pair. It was only two years earlier that I'd arrived in London with no knowledge of the written or spoken English language. Now, I was starting a new job as a nanny. It was childcare again, but I no longer had to live with the family; it was an act of liberation. I was moving into a huge Victorian house in Streatham Common in South West London. The house had nine bedrooms and fifteen housemates, including me. The housemates were a mix of people from Slovakia and the Czech Republic. Since I'd grown up in the former Czechoslovakia, it felt more like a holiday house as there were so many of us.

We had a few days of an Indian summer that autumn. I remember one particular Saturday morning I'd made plans to go shopping for new things to wear, as any twenty-something with some free pocket money would do. But as I walked towards the train station on this pleasant day, suddenly I was feeling let down by the thoughts in my head... something wasn't right. I told myself that I lived on my own, had a fairly good job and was about to buy new clothes, yet I wasn't at all happy. I looked up into the blue sky and an existential question sprang to mind: "Is this all there is in this life?" This remark ate me alive. The idea of working and spending hard-earned cash on material things felt somehow dull and empty. I couldn't find any satisfaction in the emptiness of it all. The moment felt somehow hollow.

In the meantime, back in the house a few weeks after I'd settled in, one housemate who studied psychology asked me if I'd like to meet someone with psychic abilities. I'd never heard of psychics, or mediums or clairvoyants before, so I said, "Why not?"

The room he was in was on the top floor of the house. When I walked in, an immediate feeling of warmth washed over my body, I instantly felt calm in his company. There was an eerie dim light from the few candles burning around the room. He sat in a chair across from mine and looked at me with his piercing blue eyes. He then closed his eyes and his attention moved towards my right and he asked his guides to be present by his side. It almost felt like he was having a dialogue with higher beings from somewhere else. When ready, he turned back to me and channelled the following messages from them to me.

"I see three birds in the sky... The middle one almost died. His heart stopped beating but came back again. It was very weak but he pulled through at last.

"Your grandma... I see your grandma through your eyes. She was very beautiful when she was about fourteen years old... I can see her telling stories to children... there are many children around her. Your grandma was an interesting soul. If she'd had more time she would have become a storyteller.

"She is here with us *right now*. You are *never alone*, for she is with you wherever you go... Remember that. I can see that her favourite flower was a poppy..."

The psychic then changed the topic. "There is one main long road through a valley and above the road is a hill with three crosses. There is a boy pointing a gun at a man. He looks like a soldier. I'm not sure exactly what happened here. I see two holes underground just below the crosses. They look like caves."

Then he said the following: "The only way forward for you is to use your creativity. The mundane routine doesn't do you any good, and it will kill your soul. You have to do many tasks but they can't be repetitive. You have to go along your own path. You don't need many people around. You should research spiritualism; it would give you understanding and greater purpose in life. You will achieve balance only by looking into it. Let your word be heard.

"You won't get very rich in life, but you won't be poor either. Your health is good and your diet is balanced.

"Now, your grandma is standing by your side. She's wearing something like an apron and she's pointing her hands into the front pocket on her outfit. She's telling you to put all your money aside and keep saving as much as you can because you will need it. But don't worry too much, the money will come.

"There's one man who keeps going away and then coming back again. Don't worry about men and boyfriends, someone will find you at a later stage in life when you achieve balance. Just keep finding yourself first. He is waiting for you."

And then the psychic asked me to put the palms of my hands above his.

"You have healing hands," he said. "There is heat coming from both of them… One more thing! Your grandma is telling me that you should sew the button that is in your pocket back on the jacket."

That's when I remembered. I reached in my pocket and there was the button that had fallen off my jacket that particular morning. I was speechless. I couldn't believe what was happening. I thanked him for his time. He mentioned that I should read the story of Jonathan Livingston Seagull. My mind was blown away! It was such a profound experience that it left me thinking there was so much more to life than what meets the eye. I had thought the Universe had heard my call prior to this episode, and when I asked if this was all there was in this life, I was then introduced to a man who turned everything upside down. There was a new light, a new path that I should explore unfolding in front of my eyes. It was extraordinary. How could a man I'd never met in my life speak to my grandma and see the village where I grew up? I couldn't get my head around it. After we left, I went to write everything down, and then I called my mum. Only she knew some of the things about my grandma, who had passed away a few years before. I was still a child back then.

My mother was born prematurely and was transferred into an incubator. She weighed only 3lb 15oz and the doctors at the time didn't give her much chance of survival. Her heart was very weak; they thought it was a miracle that she'd lived. From the reading of the psychic, it was clear that my mother was the middle bird, my grandma the eldest, and I was the last bird.

My grandmother had a difficult life. Her own mother died when she was only twelve years old, and being the oldest of five children, she had to support her father to help raise her younger siblings. Apart from playing the mother figure for them all, she also helped with childcare in the household of a local doctor in her town. My mother always told me that I reminded her of my grandma very much, but I was unaware until this point that she also looked after other people's children too. At the age of nineteen, my grandma married my granddad and they had six children of their own, three daughters and three sons. My grandma's house was the last one in the village next to a huge field, and in summertime it was full of red poppies. My grandmother became very ill towards the end of her life with Alzheimer's disease. She died in April 1997 aged only fifty-nine.

For someone who has never met me, the statements and the accuracy of the prophecy from this man was incredible. Now, people are sceptical about those encounters; they don't believe them. If someone had told me about such a story I wouldn't have believed them myself, not unless I'd experienced it. I was even more surprised when he saw my local village. My tiny little village has only eight hundred inhabitants, and he saw it! There is only one main road as he rightly pointed out, and above it, tucked away among the trees is a small peak with three crosses. The history or the meaning of those crosses is slightly mysterious, as not even the locals know exactly what happened there. One version says that there was an aeroplane crash during the Second World War. Another legend says that someone was killed there. There are two caves below the hilltop and another wooden cross just outside this sacred place with the year 1934 engraved on it. This is a place of sanctuary for me, and my first destination whenever I go home to see my family. The crosses aren't very visible from the main road; you wouldn't see them unless you knew they were there.

These visions from the psychic gave me new hope, new direction and a 'beacon of light' to believe that there was a reason behind all that was happening. Someone once said that it's not important which direction you take in life as long as you are growing along the way. He revealed a new path for me, towards discovery, enlightenment and trusting my destiny. Although it felt very unreal and mysterious, I was intrigued by it all. And then I remembered one more thing. They say that only with the passing of time will the truth be revealed. We might not understand 'the here and the now' of that particular moment in life, but as the time passes by, the meaning will be revealed when we are ready to understand the 'why'. With this in mind, the memory of my grandma's funeral came to the forefront of my thoughts.

I was only fourteen years old when my grandma died. I didn't have the chance to see her towards the end of her life when she was fighting the illness in hospital. On the day of the funeral, I saw her fragile body lying in the coffin. She was unrecognisable – very thin, only skin and bones, nothing like I remembered her while she was alive. It felt like she wasn't there any more. The frame of her body was like a cage, the soul, the essence was gone. As we stood above her grave in the cemetery, a strong wind started blowing. All of a sudden, I felt a presence, and a feeling of happiness entered me. I didn't understand it. Something had taken over me. I couldn't grasp the feelings within me. None of it made sense in the context of the present moment. People were grieving and yet I felt like jumping up and down with immense joy and happiness. I thought that I might be going insane.

It's a custom in my country to share lunch with the family and loved ones after the funeral. I sat across the table, watching my mother with her two sisters, each side by side, tears rolling down their faces. I had to hold back my feeling of newly encountered bliss. My emotions were such a contrast to their grief that it felt insane. It felt like watching a dark black and white grotesque, or a comedy. If in that instant I had let loose and burst into laughter I would have been looked upon as a disgraceful child, so I kept quiet. I managed to sustain my sanity. I just couldn't tell anyone. There was no other way. They wouldn't understand.

Now, according to the psychic's prophecy, my grandmother is always with me, and I believe her spirit came through on the day of her funeral. You can call me naive, a lunatic or a dreamer, but I know it was her. The shift in the energy field of my body was her soul entering mine. Our souls are eternal, they never die, they travel through space from one lifetime to another. This is a truth that I acquired through reading a book called *Many Lives, Many Masters* by Dr Brian Weiss a few years later. This man accessed the wisdom of the ascended masters while taking his patients through past life regressions, and the wisdom gained and the encounters experienced from these sessions were mind-blowing. It opened up a door to a different reality.

On a number of occasions, mostly when I travelled abroad on my own, a poppy flower would suddenly appear out of the blue. I knew it was a sign, a sign that she was with me wherever I went. This also explains the fact that I feel happy alone.

One of the books the psychic advised me to read was *Jonathan Livingston Seagull*, written by Richard Bach. It's a story of a bird, a seagull who wanted to fly higher and faster than any other bird in his flock. The rest of the seagulls were mostly concerned about flying within a familiar distance from shore to shore in search of food. Their lives were ordinary and their routine was the same every day. Jonathan, however, was different. He was obsessed with learning to fly higher and faster than any other gull had reached before. He was hard on himself, and each day he tried to break his previous flying record. He acquired such a speed that it raised an alarm among his own folk. After one such flying episode, his own parents disowned him, for they didn't want their son to break the rules and differentiate himself from his own flock of birds. Jonathan didn't understand their reaction and had nowhere else to go but to follow his own path. He met the ascended masters, teachers who become his guides. Once he'd reached his own goal, he became a master and a teacher himself. At the time of reading this story, I was immersed in the part of Jonathan's growth while wanting to learn more and more. However, towards the end of the story, I felt very disappointed with the fact that after all his efforts he was to become just a plain teacher. It didn't make much sense to me at the time. After all the hardship he had been through, I thought there would be more to life than that. But today I understand. Today I know the word 'teacher' has a very different meaning, for we are all teachers living life through our own mysteries and the acquired knowledge that we seek becomes a gift for the rest of humanity. Because the knowledge we acquire belongs to us all. It came from the Universe and it belongs back from where it originated.

***

As the year 2005 was coming to a close, I travelled home to spend time with my family. Upon my return to London towards the end of January 2006, I signed up for a short course to study 'Fashion History: The Evolution of Style' at the London College of Fashion (LCF). My determination at wanting to study this subject was stronger than ever and I decided to apply for full-time study. At the beginning of March, three weeks after the invitation was sent, I was invited for an interview. On the 9th of April 2006, I received a letter telling me that I could enrol on the Foundation Degree in Fashion Design with Marketing at the LCF in October 2006. I couldn't believe my luck. The stars were on my side!

# 2. Childhood Memories

My mother carried me in her womb as she was climbing up a ladder building a house with my dad for me and my brother. I blame my high energy levels based on this, because I must have been bounced up and down inside her stomach. We were an ordinary family of five with a simple background. Neither of my parents went to university; they worked hard to provide for us. My brother is two years older than I am and my sister came three years after that. I was the middle child. My mother often reminded me that during my christening ceremony the priest said I stared back at him with my eyes wide open, observing everything as if I already knew what was happening.

We lived in a small village in South West Slovakia under the Carpathian Mountains. My parents built their house from scratch with savings made during the communist years. It was a single-storey semi-detached house, where the left-hand side of the building looked exactly the same as the right. My dad's sister – my auntie – lived next door to us. I was never fond of such close proximity and neither was my mum. This closeness created years of a copycat relationship and amusing rivalry between my aunt and my mother as I was growing up. It might have been about new curtains, a change of front door or the shutters on windows; if one of us was doing some work on their half, the neighbour would follow. I found this very amusing and equally boring.

I have very fond childhood memories, as the village was our playground. Our house was more or less in the middle of the village, along the main road. This made our house the epicentre of the Universe. Having an older brother, younger sister, cousin next door and my best friend living a few doors away, it made this an idyllic set-up for our mischief all year round. All our playing happened outdoors, whether it was spring, summer, autumn or winter. Out in the streets, gardens, hills or forests, we felt as free as a flock of birds. Being out there in the fresh air from dawn to dusk, exploring and discovering new, barely trodden paths, climbing and swinging on ropes hanging from mighty trees, playing hide-and-seek or breaking into old windmills were our favourite things to do. The other property next door to ours was unoccupied for many years, and it was an easy target as the backyard had no fences around it. At the back of the property was a garden, and a narrow stream ran through it, but there was a steep hill further down and the gentle stream turned into a cascading waterfall that was a marvellous sight in its own right, singing its own melody. In the summertime, the pool below the waterfall was full of small fish. It was safe to jump in and cool down in the heat. In the winter months, when everything was under a blanket of snow, the waterfall transformed into an icicle cave with a curtain full of glittering light. It was a wonderful sight. I would stand there silently and wait for the sparkle from the sun and the shimmering of the light. Nature and its kingdom was the place where I felt most alive. That was my home, the purity of it all, where I felt complete freedom. Those were the golden happy days that I loved most of all.

Father was very strict though, and games were allowed only after chores were done. We had to work hard in the fields all year round to please him, and each season brought different chores. He only ever knew how to do things the old-fashioned way, which meant hard labour for us all. He wasn't changing with the times, moving ahead, and his ideas never changed. His moods altered like a see-saw and we never knew what to expect. We had to honour him, do the work and keep our mouths shut, for we were scared. I learned discipline through hard work, dignity and perseverance. Our mother filled in the gaps with her loving heart and caring nature. Every day after school, we found three plates on the table with meals made from fresh vegetables. Mum was always there. Love was never spoken about out loud, but it was felt.

When it came to education, I was the smartest one among my siblings. My brother and sister weren't blessed this way. I took pride in education and enjoyed learning new things as it made me happy to make my parents proud. All homework became my sole responsibility. I gained freedom through my independence from a young age and my parents fully supported me in every single way. And I value my upbringing to this day as it spread across many aspects of how I choose to live my life. I was a little rebellious too. My mum never said 'No' to me; she basically couldn't. Even if she disagreed, we would keep it secret from my dad to avoid causing an unnecessary fight. She knew that once her stubborn daughter set her mind to a thing or two there was no turning back. She would always say: "Go and do whatever you want, but if it doesn't work out, don't come and cry on my shoulder" – that was the warning in advance. I was a stubborn child and always did things my way at whatever cost, and my childhood was ruled by this wisdom, which was gained through my own experience. For me, it was the best way to learn.

But there was something else. Ever since I could remember I'd felt a little different from others, as if I never truly belonged. My auntie living next door helped to contribute towards this feeling. I know she resented me as I was doing better at school than her daughter. I remember one particular hot summer day my siblings and cousins and I sat on the steps in front of our house. The rest were all blue eyes, rosy cheeks and blond hair; I was the odd one out – a brunette with freckles on my cheeks that were even more visible during summertime. I can't remember who was there to take a photograph of us all, but I clearly remember the statement my auntie made about me not fitting into the tribe. I don't think it bothered me that much when she said it, but it surely went deeper than I acknowledged at the time.

Another act of refusal happened during my first Communion ceremony. Going to church every Sunday morning was a rule set by my father, as the village was strictly Catholic. It's a custom in my country that the godparents are present during this ceremony. The godparents are always family members, unlike in England, where a good family friend or any relative would do. My godfather was my dad's brother, so his wife would ultimately be the godmother. As the ceremony was coming to an end, it was a custom that the parents invited the godparents for lunch, and that's what my mother did. She's an excellent cook and was well prepared for this special occasion. However, outside the church, my godmother announced that she no longer wished to be my guardian, and in fact they decided there and then not to be part of our family any more. The icing on the cake was her comment hoping that if I did get married my dress should be a prettier version of the one I wore on that day. I was only nine years old. My dad was hit the hardest by this statement as it was his favourite brother cutting the bonds of the family. For a simple man from a village with a strong connection to his roots, this was something very difficult to overcome. It was a bizarre situation and we've never seen them since. I was only a child. My biggest regret was that I never saw her again. My godmother was something of a style icon to me. Whenever we went to visit their house she was always immaculately dressed, and I would eye her up and down and admire her style. I didn't know she was wearing a mask and behind those clothes was a heart as cold as ice. My godparents were the only people I knew that travelled to far-off countries, and this added to the mystery of a child's curiosity. They visited Melbourne in Australia, and I recall old Kodak pictures of this land down under. It felt very exotic and unusual. You must understand that this was extremely rare. In fact, I didn't know anybody else in the village that travelled so far, especially so soon after the fall of the communist years, when it was difficult to go anywhere. I heard they went off to work in Brussels soon after they rejected us as a family. Soon after this incident, my auntie next door pulled me to one side and said something that wasn't very nice to an innocent child: "See? Now you won't have a godmother, nor any presents at all…"

I was a child with an inquisitive mind who always asked 'Why?', and I was on a quest to know the truth from the very early days, and perhaps the actions of my family circle contributed towards me wanting to know the reason behind everything.

I must have been a weird child when I was a teen. My best friend and I liked to visit the cemetery in the dark. Once, at a poetry competition when I was still in my primary school years, I chose to recite one about death. It was a long poem with twelve paragraphs and each one started with the same phrase: 'When I die I want to die in May'. My literature teacher laughed at why I wanted to die so young; the answer wasn't one I could explain. I was just drawn to it. Art was another subject I excelled at, and my teacher noticed. One of my first artworks back in nursery years was a 'Dancing Forest', with trees, flowers, mushrooms and butterflies all dancing away holding hands in circles celebrating life. I ended up gifting it to my second neighbour; she couldn't have children of her own and it made her happy.

During my troubled teens I created a painting with a black line across a white frame, dividing it into two halves. The upper one was full of light that represented Heaven on Earth, but there were steps below the line, and it was very easy to slip down into the darkness. I don't recall where the source of the inspiration came from. It arrived in my brain effortlessly, without a thought in my mind; I just transferred the image onto the cardboard and wondered what it was about.

My upbringing in the village wasn't always a walk in the park. Sometimes it was far from ideal, but it taught me a lot and I wouldn't change it for the world. The natural landscape was my oasis, my escape. The people who lived there were altogether different, but they say the environment in which you grow up contributes towards your personal growth and your path. It's up to you what you choose to take from it. I believe that my soul chose my birth parents with this purpose in mind because I needed to learn lessons that would enable me to face certain challenges later in life. It helped me to see how people would act when they had hidden intentions and aspirations. I was a quiet child who liked to watch, although I never understood the meaning of it all, and for this reason I kept myself a little distant and hidden from everyone. Despite these ups and downs, I still saw myself as a happy Eastern European child. Acceptance and forgiveness are the greatest lessons of all.

# 3. Passion for Fashion

I don't recall when my calling towards fashion began but I know it's been there ever since I was a child. Perhaps my godmother planted a seed, or maybe my grandmother; she used to mend her own clothes too. Another influence came through an older sister of my best friend, who studied fashion design in Bratislava, our capital. But the funniest part is that perhaps the greatest influence on nurturing my creative streak came from my father.

This was back in the day, when I was still in my primary school years. My father was a builder who specialised in laying tiles on floors and in bathrooms. They would call him to go and work on occasional shifts in Germany. This wasn't long after the fall of the Communist Party in former Czechoslovakia. He would go with a group of friends and, as you might expect, crossing the borders wasn't an easy task as strict regulations were still in place. You were lucky if you got out from the country and then lucky again to be let in without too much questioning. 'Black Market' it was called – a bunch of Eastern European men working illegally, mostly in Austria or Germany, wanting to bring home some foreign currency to support their families. He would go for a few weeks, sometimes a month, then return and then head back again. Upon each return, my father not only brought home some 'schillings' or 'Deutsche Marks', but the highlight for me was a bin bag full of clothes from 'Tuzex'. 'Tuzex' was a network of shops with second-hand clothing from Western countries that were sold in plastic bags per weight in kilograms. Sweets in a sweetshop was nothing in comparison to this; it ignited my imagination and fed the creative streak in me. The excitement each time new stuff arrived filled my heart with joy and happiness. The ecstasy of going through these things and picking out individual pieces caused my imagination to run wild at what I could put together, either combining existing clothes or cutting them up and putting them back together in my own unique style. It was a source of pure delight. There was a brief period in my childhood when those trips took place, and sooner or later they had to slow down and then stop completely, as it was a dangerous game to play. But those bags stuffed with foreign clothes from abroad were a treasure trove for a curious little girl with scissors in her hands! I owe my creative passion and obsession with fashion to this experience from my early years. I got my first Singer sewing machine at the age of twelve. It became the best toy I ever had, and I felt over the moon at possessing one.

Upon completing my primary education, I knew my next step had to be in fashion. There were only two colleges that concentrated on fashion design and technology in Slovakia. One of them was in Bratislava, our capital. The course lasted for four years and included everything from the history of art, along with other generic subjects such as literature and maths, to weekly practical sewing lessons, figural life drawing, fashion design development and pattern cutting. To get in I had to pass entrance exams; they took only twenty students per class. I attended art classes in a county town next door to my village a year in advance to improve my figural drawing and to help build an art portfolio for the exams. As in any corrupt Eastern European country, money in someone's pocket or a contact would have helped. I never liked the fact that only those in privileged positions had a chance. My dad had a contact, so I kept my mouth shut. It certainly helped, but I was determined to succeed regardless of his friend, and I worked hard. Out of the twenty, I came second. I couldn't believe it. I still remember the feeling of pride standing outside the exam board with my result. I was so happy. I couldn't contain the feelings of bliss and joy when I saw my name. I went and bought a big bar of chocolate. Anyone who knows me also knows that I don't eat chocolate. Truth to be told, it didn't taste that good – the victory tasted better!

The four years that followed were years of dedication and

enthusiasm in my chosen field. I immersed myself in my studies. Nothing in my life was more important than to do well in this. And I did. I wasn't interested in anything else. I was a shy and introverted student. The majority of the other kids came from the capital, so I felt a little distant and tried to blend into my surroundings as opposed to rebelling and being seen. The cool kids from Bratislava socialised outside school, going to pubs and having fun during the final years of their study. I had to commute to the capital from the countryside, Monday to Friday, and never made any strong friendships, which made me feel like an outsider.

It was painful for a teenager to live in a small village where nothing ever happened. There was one bar with a disco that we attended on Saturday nights from the age of fifteen, but that was it. My best friend from childhood always dreamed of finding a boyfriend with a car so she could escape, and she did. He was the one; they married and they now have two beautiful children. I wasn't interested in boys at the time; they didn't seem important as yet. And the fact that our fashion-oriented class consisted of nineteen girls and one boy didn't help. Back in the village, I took a job distributing the local papers on the weekends to earn some pocket money as I was saving up to go for a trip abroad as soon as I graduated. The other girls I grew up with started sleeping around with the local boys. The gossip of who went off with whom intensified as we were growing up. I was losing track of these shenanigans.

I graduated with a distinction in every single subject, including my major design assignment. The theme I'd chosen for my project was called 'The Metamorphosis – A Waterfall of Ideas' with 'Woman as a Flower' as my main source of inspiration – a flower that grows from a seed and blossoms into a beautiful exotic bloom and a magnificent plant. At the peak of her beauty she would spread her seeds around her, symbolising rebirth and further evolution.

I had sleepless nights prior to the final exams. I remember the assigned tutor for this project pushed me to the edge to get me to produce the most authentic piece of art from the depth of my inner self. It was a quest for the best I could possibly give. And I know

I delivered.

Following my victory, I registered for a talent competition called Young Designer of the Year, which was running across the entire country – this was in 2001. I had hoped this competition would help me to pursue my dream of becoming a fashion designer or gain an easier entry to the Academy of Fine Arts and Design in Bratislava. My ultimate aim was to study this subject further. Unfortunately, since I didn't know the date of this competition at the time of my submission, I feared it would clash with my summer holiday upon graduation, which I'd already planned, and sadly it did. The event clashed with my two-week vacation in Italy. I had been saving up for this journey with my pocket money during the year. The trip was already booked, and there was nothing I could do to change it. My parents went to the competition in my absence and they brought home a prize for second runner-up in my name. My fellow classmate took the first prize. It was the first time my passion for fashion clashed with my desire to travel the world.

The two-week trip to Rimini along the Adriatic coast with my childhood friend, her boyfriend and my former classmate was the best thing that had ever happened to me up to that point. Before this, I'd only travelled abroad on school trips accompanied by adults, particularly my primary school teacher, who took us abroad as much as she could because she believed it would broaden our horizons, and it did. It left me feeling hungry to explore more.

During this coming of age trip, the four of us felt liberated, young and free. We were so sad when it came to an end, and my friend actually cried all the way back. When I returned home my mother said that she had never seen her daughter more beautiful and happier in her entire life so far!

# 4. Troublesome Teens

Once the trip to Italy was over and done with, harsh reality returned and the question 'What's next' was eating me alive! There was only one University of Fine Arts and Design in the capital and only one course with fashion design as the main subject. The entrance exams were fierce. They lasted for three days. Day one was known for being the toughest of them all. It involved a life portrait drawing, to eliminate those who weren't good at it. Although I was good at figural drawing, portraits weren't my strength. With the amount of creative talent that we had in Slovakia, I knew my chances were small. My parents' pockets weren't deep enough and I had no contacts among the higher echelons of the arts industry. I didn't pass the first round, so I went to try my luck at costume design at the Academy of Performing Arts instead. I was hoping this course wouldn't have as many applications. Clearly, I was wrong. There were no opportunities on the horizon.

I was young, bright, and full of hopes and ideas but with nowhere to apply them. I felt lost, but I couldn't sit still. My summer of 2001 started with me working at a carwash based out of town. I was polishing the windows of cars passing by on a motorway. In the beginning everything that's new seems exciting and fun, but once it became repetitive it turned out to be terribly boring. As a fresh graduate, I was looking for a decent job. An interview with a company that was distributing children's books into pre-schools and nurseries came up, but since it was the summer all the schools were closed and the company concentrated on 'direct' or 'cold' selling instead. It was a small brand run by a single boss who was full of himself. He had two secretaries, one sales representative and two assistants when I joined the team. He would drive us in his Skoda Octavia – his princess, as he liked to refer to his car – to new destinations in cities nearby. He dropped us off with the bulk of books to sell at the start of the day and collected us towards the end of the shift. I had to go around the streets approaching people in the main squares and in shops and offices to find potential buyers. With all my shyness as a young graduate, this was a case of 'feeling the fear and doing it anyway'. It was scary, overwhelming and liberating all at the same time. People's reactions were always reserved when we were direct selling. I got a lot of rejections and unexpected reactions, but also smiles from strangers and the odd welcoming crowd. I talked about the children's books engaging people's minds with a child's playfulness and charm. Every day was different. The whole summer was very pleasant, hot and sunny. My confidence grew by the day as I hit daily targets and beat all the others with my sales. They said I was small in size but strong in will. My plan was to have a driving licence by the end of the summer, for which I was already taking lessons, and once the schools reopened in September I was to become a full-time member of the team and carry on selling larger volumes of children's books to pre-schools and nurseries. But before the summer ended, we went on a road trip to Croatia with the team – the two sales reps, one secretary, the boss and me.

We hit the road straight after work. I don't recall the whole journey but I remember drinking loads of tequila shots with salt off my hand once we'd hit the seaside in the middle of the night. There was a massive thunderstorm that same night, and I remember eating wet grapes straight from the vine at the back of the terrace in the bar, and then I have a distant memory of driving along the road by the sea with water splashing against the windows of the car.

The morning after was very hot and the sky as clear and blue as if the storms the night before had never happened. The rest of the trip is a blur, but I'll always remember the drive back home because it could have been the last one I ever took!

The morning before we hit the road I remember sitting in the passenger's seat when my boss sprayed a fragrance by Hugo Boss into the air… and he asked what the perfume reminded me of. I was caught on the spot, and I wondered where was he leading with those remarks, and I blushed. After a few minutes I replied that perhaps it was the smell of citrus, like lemon. I didn't know what was wrong with him at the time. Today, I realise he had a massive ego and perhaps he wanted to hear how amazing he was. Or maybe he was expecting to hear that the perfume he was showing off was the sign of a strong man… or maybe he wanted something more… I don't know. All I can say is he was in denial and I wasn't there to play his games.

On the way back we were trapped in his car with him, and he was trying to show himself as the big man. He drank beer all the way, cutting the corners at full speed. If you know the Croatian coast, you also know there is a long strip of road along the edge of a cliff. At one point, a flock of sheep appeared after a blind corner. Luckily, we missed them. He held the steering wheel with one hand but with the other he was sipping one beer after another, and laughing hysterically. Terrible tunes were blaring from the stereo system. I sat in the middle on the edge of the back seat between the two other salesmen. The secretary was next to him. Terrified, none of us made a sound, but we all feared for our lives. At any minute the bend we were taking might have been our last. It was the first time that I'd feared for my life. My father wasn't even aware I was there! The secretary was an angel though. I don't know how, but after a few hours she managed to convince him she should take over the steering wheel. He never allowed anyone to drive his princess, especially a woman. We were relieved at last!

I got my driving licence at the end of that summer but I never started selling books to schools and nurseries. I don't remember the exact circumstances when I left the company, but one morning sticks out in my memory. The boss had a picture of the Twin Towers in a frame on the wall in the office. The morning I recall was 11th September 2001. The focus of the picture on the wall was a little bit of history. And so was the job for me.

Shortly after this episode, I found myself selling life insurance across the capital. I was cold-calling again. One day I entered the office of a company where I met a middle-aged woman sitting behind a computer screen. She told me that soon I would find a nine-to-five job and then meet a man, settle down, have kids and a house and ten years would pass by and life would be the same every single day… just like that.

Woooow, hold on! I thought to myself. That was a recipe for misery! In my mind that was the ultimate death. I knew it would destroy my creative soul. It wasn't the path I wanted so I quit the job and said goodbye. From the beginning till the end, it was everything I didn't believe in!

Winter was coming. It was six months after my graduation and there were no prospects on the horizon. There was a brand new shopping centre called Polus City Centre in the capital. I was offered a job as a sales assistant in a small boutique. I was partially in my element at last. The shop had a selection of ladies' wear purchased in France and the business was doing well; at least, it looked like it was. The few weeks towards Christmas Eve were a busy period and the shop was open from 10 am to 10 pm every day throughout December. But then I heard news from neighbouring concessions that our owners were going to close down after New Year's Eve. However, staff, including me and the manager, weren't informed about such a closure at all. In fact, the owners hardly ever came in during opening times so we never had the chance to ask. The rumours intensified as the year came to an end. My manager was a tough woman. She'd raised three kids while her husband was in prison for domestic violence. She wasn't one to be messed about and decided to act on our behalf. On the last day of the month, we deducted our salaries from the month's takings and never came back to work again! That was at the end of December 2001.

Soon after the incident, I received a letter from a lawyer of the company and I was called to a police station for questioning. I told them the truth. In fact, I had been working illegally as my month trial period had run out in the first week of November and my contract had never been extended by the employers. The police didn't take our well-earned cash back. At the end of the day, we only took the amount based on the hours and shifts worked. I have never heard of the boutique owners or the lawyer again. Although it does leave a mark if someone calls you into a police station suggesting you are a criminal at the age of nineteen.

I needed a break and a change of scenery after that. My former college friend with whom I travelled to Italy now lived in Prague with her boyfriend and their pet rabbit. I went to visit them. It was my first time in the 'golden city of a hundred spires', but it was only a temporary escape. Upon my return, harsh reality began to sink in. I felt lost in my life. I didn't know what to do or where to go next. A real deep feeling of helplessness spread through me. I felt depressed and broken-hearted. I couldn't find a job that would satisfy my needs or help me to progress in my desired direction. Slovakia felt somehow small and unsupportive of the younger generation. I'd lost confidence in the system and in the hope that anything would change. The unemployment rate at the time was on the rise. For a sensitive soul with dreams and hopes for a fresh beginning, there was nothing, absolutely nothing, for me to do at the time.

Was I happy? No! The once happy Eastern European child was feeling trapped in its own Universe. The golden years of childhood were truly gone. How I yearned to be that free bunny running across fields chasing butterflies carelessly once again! It all made sense now; adulthood was grey and mundane. I remember visiting job centres and seeking unemployment benefits. I had to find a new direction. That feeling of helplessness… a young person full of life and eagerness to learn and to reach higher achievements was burning inside me. I decided I was done with Slovakia and that I would leave my birth country in order to find happiness elsewhere. There was no other way out. I had to leave it behind.

At the time I didn't know anything about numerology, but today I have some insight because of Joanne Walmsley's numerology. When a number is repeated, this is a message from the angels that follow your path. In my case, the number two was repeated on the date of my departure five times. It resonated with ancient wisdom and the influence of faith and trust that everything will work out for the best in its own divine timing. On the 22nd of February 2002, I left for Germany to work as an au pair.

# 5. A Year in Germany

The village in Germany was tiny. It felt as small as the one I'd just escaped. The nearest town was Alzey, set in the region of Rheinland-Pfalz Gebiet in western Germany. The family had three sons, and I was to spend a year with them to help with the childcare and contribute towards the smooth running of the household. My German was poor to start with, although I learned the grammar at school. Through my own experience, I found that learning a foreign language while being thrown into an environment where the tongue is being spoken is the best way for it to sink in. You have no choice. First, I learned through listening. Although I attended extra evening classes at a college in Alzey, I would call the mother of the boys my primary teacher. She was from the northern region of Germany, where they spoke 'Hochdeutsch' without any dialect. Because of her northern origin, she was an outsider in the village and had hardly any friends in the neighbourhood. Each day after lunch she told me how her day went and all the drama about her impossible boss at the pharmaceutical company that she worked for. The father had run away from his family at the age of sixteen after he'd fallen out with his father. It seemed that his relatives were very much the same as my father's side of the family, where intrigues and jealousy were a daily occurrence. He was a successful businessman and the director of a construction and building company. The house the family lived in was built by him. I lived beneath them in a basement flat all of my own with a separate entrance, and my afternoons were pretty much free. There wasn't much going on apart from my daily routine. You have to understand I had no access to the internet in 2002 and I had no car and no friends. In my spare time, I was mostly alone.

The nearest town didn't have many interesting shops with clothes either, the majority of it was boring sportswear. Back in my flat, I listened to Robbie Williams' album *Escapology* endlessly. Mind you, I didn't understand the lyrics. The thought of being trapped in yet another tiny village where nothing ever happened made me want to escape really badly. I dreamed of being in a big city because I knew that even if I didn't know anyone, there would always be something to do or something to see.

Before I left home my mother gave me a piece of advice to not show everything I can do. She wanted to protect me so people wouldn't take advantage of my skills. I thought she was right at the time but I couldn't help myself. Today I know she was wrong, as acquired knowledge belongs to us all. To keep myself occupied I started helping with extra chores around the house just out of boredom. On a trip to Ikea with the mother, we bought some furnishing fabrics and I convinced her to buy a sewing machine too. Soon I was making pillowcases for garden furniture, painting fences, mending ripped trousers for the boys or anything else that needed altering. I turned the other room of my basement flat into a studio and started painting too. My creativity was always there. It kept me going. I painted a large artwork of sunflowers under the sea, calling it an 'Oasis'. I was partially inspired by Vincent Van Gogh's *Sunflowers*, but I admired the impressionistic and idealistic smooth lines of Salvador Dali too. Perhaps this 'Oasis' was my 'appeal' for a more beautiful existence or a reflection of the 'undersea bubble' I lived in. I gifted it to the family. They had it beautifully framed and hung it in their living room.

My life as an au pair was fairly simple, although the boys did give me a hard time too. Sometimes they would shout at me to go away. I knew I didn't belong, but when it came from an innocent child with a furrowed brow and a voice full of anger – that seriously hurt me! I was still a big child myself and had nowhere else to go, at least not back then, but it got better over time. I was the only au pair in the village and the kids might not have fully understood why all of a sudden there was an extra element within their family who wasn't a sibling. I didn't have any friends there until I met another Slovakian girl a couple of months later. She wasn't an au pair as such. Instead of children, she looked after three dogs for a lesbian couple in a neighbouring village a few kilometres away. We would spend some weekends together when the pair of them weren't around. The Slovak girl was twenty-five years old. Her mother cried for her daughter to come home every day on the phone. This raised a red flag in my head as my mother never called. I had no contact with my family until about six months into my stay. I was still only nineteen at the time and thought that nobody missed me. I asked her why she didn't call more often. She explained that she didn't want to create a feeling of neediness in me, and by not calling it made me a stronger person. It was an interesting way of looking at it and I liked the thought of it. The twenty-five-year-old soon went back home to Slovakia and luckily for me she was replaced with another Slovak girl who was a better friend.

We started going out more in the new year and even attended some local discos in neighbouring villages, but before that, I went home to visit my family for Christmas. I travelled to Slovakia by a coach that took a couple of hours on the motorway. I remember sitting on the bus listening to Chris Rea's 'Driving Home for Christmas' and all the other cheesy songs feeling joyful and happy ahead of the festive season. In that moment, a thought crossed my mind: I wished I could understand all the lyrics. And it *hit* me right at that moment! Now that I understood German, I wanted to learn to speak English too. And I asked myself what the point of having dreams was if we're not going to make them happen? All of a sudden there was a new seed planted in my mind and a new goal to consider.

Back in Germany in January 2003, I bought a book *English for Self-Learners*. I started with vocabulary and slowly worked my way through the grammar. It was a slow process, boring at times, but I kept pushing myself to do it.

In the spring I attended some parties with my new friend and soon I met my first boyfriend. But then I found out he was a drug addict dependent on heroin and cocaine. He was twenty-two years old, an auto mechanic specialising in the repair of large vehicles and lorries, but otherwise he was lost. All his friends were doing it. What a waste of youth, I thought. Deep sigh. Losing and drowning oneself in chemicals that caused a dysfunctional idiotic perception of reality... I didn't see the point in it at all. I only encountered drugs once, when inhaling weed through a home-made gravity bong on New Year's Eve back in Bratislava when I was about seventeen. I remember sitting above a kitchen sink holding the cupboard doors imagining I had wings! It was a funny thing, but hard drugs weren't something I'd had such close contact with previously. I only knew to stay away from them.

After our first date he announced that he was only ever interested in the physical experience. That was fine with me; it was about time! He thought I was an angel when we made love for the very first time, although that statement might have been influenced by external substances. Surprisingly, he could be rather caring and sweet when not affected by drugs, and we enjoyed each other's company. But then there were times when I didn't know how to handle certain situations I found myself in. Once, we drove to a field in the middle of the night. I can't recall whether it was a needle or the white powder he was about to indulge in, but I was warned that the outcome would either go for the better or for the worse. The latter was the case this time. He started trembling, his eyelids slipped upwards and his body was shaking, and he seemed as if he was about to lose it completely. He was moving unsteadily like a monster that had just had a fit. It was terrible to watch. I can't recall how it all ended, but I had to wait there until the side effects subsided and then drive him back home. It was yet another lesson for me to learn from and to avoid repeating at any cost!

To my surprise, after dating for a while, he started getting emotional and telling me he was falling in love. I regarded this with reservation as I knew it wasn't something I was interested in long term. I only got to know him three months before my departure, and I was leaving the country soon anyway, which was a relief. Three days before my departure he started crying. Even the parents of the boys were amused at how hard he'd fallen for me. He had a stutter

25

that got worse, and on the very last day I saw him he could hardly speak at all. He promised he would get off drugs and buy me an engagement ring if I stayed. I was scared! I wasn't sure if it was because of what he said about the ring or the love he felt. It was interesting to watch. I kept true to my feelings and stayed calmer than he did. I had no plans to lose my freedom like this, and the desire to learn more was still very strong in me. He messed with my head but I knew I didn't feel the same. I'd never seen anybody in such an emotional mess; it was a real turn-off.

When I left, as I sat in the father's BMW speeding on the motorway away from him, I felt freedom once again. As I watched the world go by from the window of the car, I felt sad about leaving the German family behind as I'd grown very close to them. Once at the coach station, the father and I said our farewells and I realised that the bond we'd created over time had made it seem like I was the daughter he'd always wished for but never had. I haven't had the chance to see the family again.

*** 

Upon my return home, everything was as if I'd never left. But I already had something planned: a week after my arrival I was going to fly to Egypt. My former college friend, who had previously lived in Prague, had been plotting this trip while I was still living in Germany. Ancient Egypt was one of my favourite subjects during our classes in the history of art. Being able to travel there and to see one of the Seven Wonders of the World with my own eyes was to be another incredible experience.

The best part of this trip was the excursion to see the pyramids at Giza and to pay a visit to the Valley of the Kings in Luxor. The most memorable thing for me was entering the individual tombs through the narrow catacombs. I was amazed by how much light there was all around us! I always thought it would be dark after entering the long, deep, narrow tunnels, but everything was as light as if the sunshine penetrated through the walls right deep inside. I kept a little rock I found. Ancient Egyptians believed that life in the physical body is as important as the afterlife. Those tombs were built for a ceremony in which they would proceed with mummification, which facilitated the soul's reincarnation into the afterlife. The more powerful the pharaoh, the more artefacts and material goods they laid next to him. How the pyramids were built remains a mystery. I had to pinch myself to believe I was there. I could tick this off my bucket list at the age of twenty.

\*\*\*

Upon my return home, my mother had a love letter for me. It was from my troubled German boyfriend, who I now labelled as part of my past. In the outpouring of his feelings and his broken heart, he said he was willing to move to my country and live somewhere in a caravan! In the meantime, I already had a different plan and had signed up with an au pair agency to flee my motherland for a second time. England was my target this time. I knew I wanted to go to London; I wanted to be at the epicentre of a big city where everything was happening.

My college friend decided to go to the USA. She left for the Big Apple in September 2003, and the next time I saw her was in the Waldorf Astoria on Park Avenue in New York seven years later. I managed to leave Slovakia for the second time around in October 2003. I still recall the question of the officer at the British Embassy in Bratislava upon my visa request. He couldn't grasp why I wanted to go to England, especially as I'd never learned English at school. For me it was simple, I wanted to learn to speak the language. Slovakia was joining the European Union in May 2004, the next spring, so no further paperwork for EU nationals living in the UK was required. Today, as I'm writing this, this is subject to change as 'Brexit' and its negotiations are the heated topic of every discussion in the press. The future is uncertain...

# 6. Au Pair in London

## Guest Family No. 1

I still remember my dad, my mother and my tearful sister standing at the coach station Mlynské Nivy in Bratislava before my farewell. And I still remember the feeling of not knowing what would happen next. That feeling of excitement, adventure, mixed emotions, and the question 'What's next' was hanging in the air. I just knew that the only way was forward; whatever will be, will be. Looking back now, it's easier to be brave when you're young, careless and free. I was twenty years old and had absolutely nothing to lose. People always asked whether I was scared. No, I wasn't scared, despite not knowing a single soul in London or England. Somehow I never felt completely alone. The inner voice had been there ever since I could remember.

After a strenuous twenty-four-hour overnight bus journey through Austria, Germany, Belgium and France, we reached the port of Calais and took a ferry to Dover. I don't recall what I imagined I would see in the land of new possibilities, but the roads through the countryside from Dover to London looked like anywhere else, only everything was under a big grey cloud. I arrived at Victoria Coach Station in the afternoon on the 17th of October 2003. I had the address of my host family on a piece of paper and my mission was to find a black cab to take me to this address in South West London. We drove around Earlsfield for a good half an hour as the cabbie couldn't find it. There was no GPS back then, only the good old A–Z map.

The destination was found at last, and a heavily pregnant

woman stood in the doorway and an angelic boy with curly blond hair and big blue eyes appeared by her side. The mother was due to deliver twins in two weeks' time. The boy was three years old. For the next couple of months, I was more or less housebound with this lot.

Once the babies were born, the hours in the day blended into weeks, then months, and every day felt the same. As an au pair, you're supposed to work no longer than twenty-five hours per week, five hours a day. My shifts were slightly different due to the nature of the situation I found myself in. The main purpose of being an au pair overseas is to attend classes to learn the foreign language alongside your duties. However, since I arrived in the middle of the term in October, I had to wait until January when the next course in college was due to start. In the meantime, I was pretty much with the mother, the twins and the boy from 7 am to 7 pm from Monday to Friday, full-time. The dad was a city worker and the mother needed all the help possible.

At the start, I had to entertain the little three-year-old while the mother fed the babies. I found the routine terribly boring. I'm even bored now writing about it all, but it was part of my journey and necessary for further personal growth. The house felt like a medieval cave where you performed the same rituals over and over again. We got on quite well despite the language barrier; it was hard for me to interact at this stage as my English was non-existent. I used my dictionary a lot. It was a very difficult time for everyone involved. The three-year-old boy was the centre of attention before the babies were born. Once they came along he often cried in despair, shouting that he hated them. It's a usual reaction among toddlers, being envious of newborn babies, and he had a double act to deal with all at once!

One evening I found the mother weeping on her husband's shoulder when he returned from work. We all had to pull through. I was unhappy because it wasn't fair to take the burden of the full-time shifts that were given to me. They were much longer than what was written in my contract with the agency and my money didn't reflect that.

The long dark winter days with hardly any sun didn't help; most of the time it was overcast and grey. One afternoon, during one of our outings with the babies, somewhere in Clapham Junction, I overheard two girls in a shop speaking Slovakian. The first thought entering my mind was whether to approach them or not. I decided to act. I ran up to them like a little puppy desperate to play for the very first time. It was about two months after my departure from home and I hadn't spoken to or heard anyone else speaking my mother tongue. The girls looked me up and down, probably wondering why I was interrupting their conversation; I must have looked desperate, and I excused my behaviour explaining that they were the first Slovakian people I had come across in the city since I'd arrived. They both worked as au pairs in Battersea, near Clapham. We swapped numbers and stayed in touch.

***

It took me some time to see Big Ben, the Houses of Parliament and discover Trafalgar Square. Only then did I realise how enormous London was and the fact that the family I lived with was based in Zone 3, which is quite far away from the City in Zone 1. Christmas was slowly approaching and I wasn't going home. It was my first Christmas spent away from my own family and I felt a little sad.

I don't recall the exact timeframe of the next incident with the guest family, however I do know it was coming up close to the festive season in the wintertime. The baby boy used to have a colic reaction each time after his formula milk and he would scream uncontrollably for a good two hours, if not more, after he was fed. This, I learned, is a usual occurrence with babies in the early phase of feeding and we just had to get on with it. One evening, however, during such a rage, he started turning purple instead. It was scary; he had breathing difficulties. The mother was worried sick. We called 999. The dad hadn't got home from work yet when the ambulance turned up and took them to hospital. I stayed put, together with the other two waiting for the dad to turn up. The mother and the baby boy stayed in the hospital for a few days.

It was during this time that I decided I wanted a pay rise and I thought I needed to bring this up before the start of the next year. It occurred to me, after talking to the other two girls from Battersea, that my duties involved many more hours in comparison to their chores, and for much lower pay. I didn't mind working full-time as long as the wage was fair, but it wasn't. I brought this up with the parents a few days after this hospital incident and was called cold-hearted and cruel. This confrontation created a crack in the relationship that proved beyond repair.

I decided to spend Christmas Eve with the two girls in Battersea making traditional Slovakian meals like we did back home. The atmosphere in the house had cooled down a little the day after, and I experienced my first traditional English Christmas with the host family on Boxing Day. It ended up being a lovely experience despite the confrontation earlier.

***

As usual, five days after New Year was my birthday, and I was turning twenty-one. That evening I went babysitting for the family next door. I later learned that their five-year-old twin brothers were adopted as the couple couldn't have children of their own. They seemed like really lovely, genuine people. My host family must have told them about my special day as they brought me a small cupcake with one lit candle before they left. I was never really that bothered about my birthdays in general and only learned much later that twenty-one is kind of a big deal in the UK.

***

In the new year, the parents accommodated my request for more money and fired their cleaner. It meant not only would I be cleaning their house but I also had to start cleaning the mother's brother's flat down the road during my lunch break. I had to work hard for whatever I wanted in life. But once I started to attend my evening classes in early January, something shifted and I was happier. It

31

became the highlight of my week as it was terribly exciting to be sitting in a classroom with so many people of different nationalities. This diversity is what's fascinating about living in a multicultural city such as London.

The course was at South Thames College in Tooting and the class I attended wasn't for beginners any more. Once I signed up and passed an entry test they rated my abilities as an advanced speaker, despite this course being the first official English class I'd ever taken. My language skills must have improved within the family environment I'd lived in. I first learned through listening again, although I definitely wasn't at the stage where I could have a full-on conversation just yet.

The downside of starting to understand more through my sharp listening and observant nature was that I overheard things I wish I hadn't heard. Once, I heard a conversation between the mother and her friends about their perception of the life of Eastern European girls; in their eyes, we had no education and came to the UK to learn to speak English so we could marry English men and settle down. This was heartbreaking for me; I hadn't come here with the intention to marry, nor to marry rich for that matter, or to marry at all. I came here because I wanted to learn and expand as an individual, and the price of being so far from my own relatives was high. After I heard these English ladies speaking of us 'poor little girls' it made me angry with rage. Just for the record, the educational system in Slovakia and other Eastern European countries is higher if not better in terms of quality and level of education than in the UK. Primary and secondary education is compulsory and free for everyone, regardless of social status or class, unlike in England. Those are the things that I had to pretend I'd never heard. It made me very angry and sad at the same time. I was mad with fury, wanting to scream in rage to prove them wrong. Sadly, I didn't have the vocabulary to do so at the time! I just had to swallow it and carry on. Deep sigh!

Life in the family and the routine in the new year carried on in the same way. For the whole eight months of my stay, the babies, the mother, the boy and I were inseparable. I questioned my existence and wondered what my next step should be. I was supposed to stay for a year, but it somehow came to an abrupt end. Once there's a split like that you can't take it back. My unhappiness was caused by the fact that we knew I was cheap labour for them, and it wasn't going to change.

At the beginning of the summer I started to look for a new host family elsewhere and informed the parents about my intentions ahead of time. It was also coming up to my holiday for two weeks, for which my flights were already booked. Before I left for my vacation, the mother of three turned to me and announced that by looking elsewhere I didn't deserve the love of their children and there was no need for me to come back again. That was the end of my first au pair experience in London. I have seen her and the kids once in a playground and then a few years later in the Earlsfield library while I was looking after other people's kids. I said hello. She ignored me and hardly made eye contact.

## Guest Family No. 2

I flew home on the 5th of June 2004 and came back on the 20th of June as originally planned. During this two-week vacation back home I researched Gumtree endlessly for a new au pair opportunity to secure my return to London, and I found one just in time. It was with a family of five living in Streatham near the Common. The mother was a freelance writer and worked from home, but occasionally she had to go to meetings in town. The dad was hardly ever there. I heard he worked on shifts somewhere on a boat. They had a girl, six, a boy, five, and a baby girl a little bit older than the twins. Since the older two were at school, I mostly spent my time in sole charge of the little one. I had free time in the afternoon, the hours weren't bad, and I was still able to attend my English class once a week at the college in Tooting.

This second family looked lovely from the outside, but there were deep scars on the inside. The dad was apparently having affairs, and whenever he came home, he and the wife argued a lot. The kids often misbehaved and never listened to what they'd been told. I felt sorry for the mother tackling it all by herself. The kids had no respect for the parents, and with the father's absence, there was no balance in the household.

One particular morning I was asked to drop off the older two kids at school and bring the baby girl along as both parents had to leave before 9 am. I thought I could certainly handle this and so did the parents as they had faith in me. But the situation got out of my hands, and as soon as the parents left, the six-year-old started playing tricks and manipulating the boy.

They ran upstairs and started jumping up and down on their parents' bed shouting there was no chance I was taking them to school that day. They ran from bedroom to bedroom as I was chasing them all over the house and my patience was evaporating. The pressure was on to make sure it all ran smoothly that morning, but it wasn't a good start. The two-year-old girl was left alone waiting downstairs in a pushchair, though I knew she shouldn't be left alone.

This chasing game went on for good forty-five minutes, if not more, and I was freaking out as I already knew we wouldn't make it to the school on time. After a while, I managed to convince the boy to come downstairs, but the girl was the difficult one to handle at the time. Somehow I managed to get her to the bottom of the stairs and forced to put her shoes on, but she ran off again. It wasn't funny. My patience had evaporated by this stage. I managed to get her down a second time around, but as she ran off again my hand flew into the air and landed on her cheek! I slapped her! Everything went quiet. I took them to school in silence with no further hassle. Of course, we were already late. Little did I know that slapping a child could lead me to prison in the UK.

When the parents returned home I complained about their offspring's misbehaviour and the irresponsibility of their daughter. Kids have to have respect from their parents in my country, and if a little bit of punishment for being naughty fixed this, then so be it! That's how I was brought up, the only way I knew.

So the mother went to tell her daughter off, and when the daughter told her mother that I'd smacked her on the cheek, she couldn't believe what her child told her. Lies were a regular occurrence in this household, it seemed. The values in this family were completely twisted.

The parents called me downstairs to have a chat. The mum asked me if what her daughter had said was true. I acknowledged it; there was no reason to say otherwise; I don't do lies. I explained that her daughter had been out of control and I'd found her difficult to handle, and towards the end of it I'd lost patience and raised my hand to her. She was a little brat – I didn't say that out loud, of course. I just acknowledged what happened and stayed quiet.

That's when the father stood up and said that if it was up to him I would be out the door right that minute! It didn't hit me as to why. I didn't understand his statement. That's when I heard for the very first time that hitting children in the UK is illegal. The mother was more forgiving and allowed me to stay until Saturday of the following week. This was just one month after my arrival into this family in Streatham and my second experience in the UK as an au pair. What doesn't kill you makes you stronger! After that week, I wished them well and thanked them for having me. Inside, I felt relieved. The Universe was telling me they weren't my kind of people.

## Guest Family No. 3

That week had been pretty intense. I went straight on Gumtree to research new au pair opportunities, as I only had a week to find a new host family. The thought of not knowing if I had somewhere to lay my head at the end of the day was terrifying, and the idea of being left on the street seemed very real. It must have been the most frightening thing that had happened to me living in this country. I certainly didn't want to end up back in Slovakia! I had to pull up my socks and fight again, but luck was on my side.

I found a new contact and went for an interview that week on the Thursday and I moved into the home of a wealthy family near Richmond over the weekend. What a relief! It was an enormous house halfway along Church Road near Ham Common that led to

Richmond Park. It used to have wooden toilets from the 1920s and was later demolished. The father of the family was originally from Germany, but his surname carried the hint of the Eastern European. That's how I knew. I knew the minute I saw the name that the Universe had listened to my despair and had once again sent a messenger and I was safe. Later I learned that the father's grandfather had emigrated from Bohemia, former Czechoslovakia, during the war and settled down in Germany.

The mother was South African, very loving and kind. They had three boys between four and ten years of age and a happy baby girl with a cheeky smile. In contrast to the previous guest family, the parents here were respected, the children well behaved and rules were followed. The mother had immense admiration for her husband, who had left Germany with nothing and built his career in a foreign country from scratch. I learned that he worked in the fashion industry as a buyer for a well-known clothing brand with its head office based in Oxford Street. You can tell that the relationship they had and the family environment they created for their children was very safe and stable. Although the father worked endless hours and didn't come home until very late at night, their marriage was strong. As fate had it, the mother learned the German language at university, not knowing that's where her future husband would come from. She revealed that it was her husband's vision to have a big family as he would have hated to come home at night into an empty house; he certainly knew how to create one.

The summer was spent in an enormous garden at the rear of the property with lots of trees you could easily get lost in. The little baby girl was adorable, a real bundle of joy to be with, and she never cried. I was happy there, although there was the problem that, apart from being with a family I clicked with, I was cut off from the rest of the city, and in my free time I was terribly bored once again.

Most of my afternoons were spent alone until I learned that two of my Slovakian friends, with whom I went to primary school, were staying in London during the summertime. It felt surreal to have them so close, and the timing was just right! I used to sit next to them in a classroom and we wouldn't talk since we were all equally shy. Now both of my friends studied economics at university in Slovakia, and during their summer break they looked after kids in London to improve their language skills. My friends had also their university friends in town, and together we formed a group of five or six. During the week we were busy, but the weekends belonged to us. It was the hottest summer that I'd experienced in London since I'd arrived and that summer belonged to us. Being far away from home – young, careless and free – we danced like we owned the nights and stayed up until the wee hours of the morning. Sundays were hangover days and girly gatherings as we laughed about the encounters from previous nights. For two months' straight I looked forward to those weekends like an excited little child. I didn't question at the time what a blessing it was to have my friends from home in town, it just happened to be that way! Today, I know that the Universe must have conspired for me to enjoy myself at twenty-one at last; it felt like heaven had sent them to me, especially after all the hardship I had been through since I'd arrived. The year 2004, that had started off so dark and grey, turned out to have a rainbow full of colour at last. Having close friends around had never felt so good!

But I knew this episode would come to an end. My girls had to leave at the end of summer and I had to evaluate my next step. I felt terribly valued in this family in Richmond and there was mutual respect on both sides. However, this place was too safe and there was no growth for me. I knew I had to leave because of the location of the house as I felt terribly cut off from the rest of the world, and burying myself in a beautiful house with the stunning surroundings of Richmond Park would have been great for some, but I heard the call of wanting to be nearer the city, interacting with young people and learning at the same time. I had experienced this situation once already in Germany and so this was no longer working for me. I was much more concerned about what my next steps would be and my personal growth going forward. The family thought I was making a big mistake, but I felt I was following my inner vocation.

There was an opportunity on the horizon. Since one of my friends was leaving her host family in Earlsfield at the end of summer, I would be able to fill in her shoes as they were looking for someone who could stay for at least a year. Funnily enough, this was a stone's throw away from my first guest family with the baby twins, and their garden was facing the kitchen window of the mother's brother, where I used to do cleaning once a week – the irony of one's destiny, or a simple coincidence…

But before I could move there was a little hiccup. Since I'd made the decision and informed the Richmond folks about my plans, they'd started looking for a new au pair replacement and they found one immediately, before my proposed departure date. My friend in Earlsfield wasn't leaving until the end of September, so there was a three-week period where I had nowhere to stay. The South African mother, being very helpful and kind, asked around her friends, and for three weeks I went to live temporarily with a family of five in East Sheen.

The farewell in Richmond was an emotional one; it brought tears to the mother's eyes. They were so lovely inside and out, it was hard to part. I remember filling my suitcases when the kids brought me some garment bags to help pack my clothes; they were happy for me to use them or throw them in the bin. Clutching those bags close to my chest, my thoughts flashed back to a memory of my long-forgotten fashion dream – my present journey felt miles away from that. It felt terribly sad throwing them away, as if something has gripped my heart or something had died.

## Guest Family No. 4

The family in East Sheen were English and had three boys. The eldest son had brain damage and was restricted to a wheelchair. The arrangement was mostly to help the mother with her sons during the morning. They already had a part-time nanny from Argentina who looked after the boy in the afternoon. The two of them had created a very special bond during the year. I was new to this; it was a different experience to help look after a child with a disability compared to my previous experiences with children. I could tell he felt discomfort and frustration in my company, as I misinterpreted his needs and behaviour occasionally. We didn't know each other enough and he became aggressive at times. I had immense respect for the parents, who were incredibly strong individuals with a relaxed manner and full acceptance of the situation they were in. As fate had it, the mother was trained as a paediatric neurologist who could take full care of her son. The Universe had seemingly prepared her to deal with the condition of her child, yet although we can cope with almost everything in life if we set our minds to it, seeing your child suffer must be the hardest thing to deal with of all.

My three weeks' stay with them came to an unpredictable end a few days ahead of my departure date. I was asked to leave because I had a cold sore on my lip. This is when I learned about the family tragedy and how the oldest boy had become paralysed. He was born as a perfectly healthy child. It happened due to an innocent grandmother's kiss; she had contagious herpes that played a major role in his destiny. It was heartbreaking to hear. I understood their worry and left. After further research, I learned that this virus is most contagious in the first two weeks of the baby's birth, when their immunity is still very weak. Sometimes neonatal herpes will only affect the baby's eyes, mouth or skin and they will make a complete recovery, but in severe situations the virus can spread to a baby's organs or brains, and in worse-case scenarios it can be fatal.

## Guest Family No. 5

At the end of September 2004, I was back in Earlsfield. The number on the door was the same as the year I was born, a simple synchronicity. The family was English and had four children. They were very excited that I was joining them as we already knew each other through my friend who by now had left the country. The older kids were at school full-time. My responsibility was for their two-year-old girl, from morning time until 4 pm. The parents had a very social lifestyle and a relaxed approach towards the upbringing of their kids. The house was always full and buzzing with happy vibes, and I was made to feel part of their family. There was only one challenge straight from the start. Three weeks into my stay the parents travelled to South Africa for two weeks, leaving their offspring behind. It was, as you can imagine, a great responsibility to start with, and I passed this challenge, falling into bed every night exhausted. Once they were back, everything fell into place. I'd found a good base, and life became more settled for the year ahead.

\*\*\*

That autumn I met my first English boyfriend, who was originally from Liverpool. He found me on the dance floor in a nightclub in Piccadilly. There was an instant mutual connection, and for the rest of the night the two of us became inseparable. He was training as an army officer at the Royal Military Academy at Sandhurst and came down to London on rare occasions as the training was very strict and his outings were limited. We kept in touch for over two years. I saw him sporadically, sometimes only once every two or three months. He used to say that I was too clever to look after children and should study at university instead. The idea of studying in England had never crossed my mind, thinking there was no way I could afford it. Today, I strongly believe that everyone who crosses our path in life happens to be there for a reason, and although our relationship was leading nowhere, this young man had a role to play in my life, for he planted a seed of reassurance, that if I wanted to study in England I could. He had faith that an Eastern European girl like me would do well in his native land, and for that, I am grateful to him.

Towards the end of the year, in December 2004, I took an exam for a First Certificate in English for Speakers of Other Languages (ESOL) by the University of Cambridge. I was one year into my time in the UK.

\*\*\*

In January 2005, I started playing with the idea of wanting to study fashion further in London. I decided to sign up for a portfolio preparation course at Central St Martins and applied for a full-time Fashion Design Womenswear course there. I knew about this school from back home, where I learned about Alexander McQueen and John Galliano, both graduates from CSM who inspired my own journey as both came from humble beginnings. I thought that if I was to follow my dream I had to try the best of the best to gain an entry into the industry. However, at the end of spring, I received a letter from Central St Martins saying that they wouldn't proceed with an interview. I wasn't good enough for them, but I thought I should try harder the following year.

One of my friends came back to London the following summer again. She made a statement that hurt like an arrow through my heart as she questioned my endless journey to nowhere being an au pair. Those notions of truth usually come from your closest friends, those who really care, but I didn't want to hear it at the time because it hurt too much, because I have tried, but it didn't work out and I didn't know how to change the situation any better at the time. There was nothing on the horizon in my life for another year to come. I was simply stuck.

On the 6th of July 2005, there was an announcement that London was to host the Olympic Games in the summer of 2012. London and Great Britain went wild with euphoria. Then, a day later, on the 7th of July 2005, the celebration was silenced by the London bombings. The city had become a major target for a terrorist attack where fifty-two people were killed and hundreds were injured. The whole nation went into a silent despair.

On that day I was visiting a friend in Wimbledon who worked as a nanny and looked after a two-year-old whose mother went for a meeting that morning in Edgware Road. Edgware Road was one of the places where a bomb exploded. Her phone was dead; we couldn't get hold of her. The question of whether she was alive hung in the air – it was terrifying. Luckily, she was safe. Mobile coverage after the attack was unavailable due to the emergency services shutting down public access to the network. But fifty-two people never came home that day. The thought of innocent families being torn apart by bombers who cared nothing about the lives of others was excruciating. I stared at the news on the TV feeling emotionally bereft.

After few days it hit me, just like that… I had to express my feelings from being unable to talk and transfer it into something tangible to filter my emotions. I poured my heart into an art-collage, imagining what it was like being trapped inside a Tube carriage. I used the newspapers with press coverage of the attack, gold acrylic paint and a pencil to draw nine figures trapped in the scene and covered in blood; somewhere in the corner the date 7/7/2005 was stamped. I moved with it many times across London. The 49x35-inch frame never hung on the wall. The reaction from various flatmates wasn't always positive towards that 'bloody painting'. I started looking at it in a different light over the span of those years. It reminded me that we are here only once and we should embrace our existence on this Earth as we don't know when it will come to an end. Last time I saw it was in a house in Norbury in South West London. The painting is now gone and I don't know its whereabouts.

**London Bombings**

In late summer, I had the intention of finding a full-time live-out nanny job to earn more money and to save in order to be able to study. The family in Earlsfield was very supportive and understanding of my plans. Childcare was the only job I had experience of, so being a full-time nanny was the only way forward.

Towards the end of August, an opportunity came knocking on my door. One of my Slovakian friends was moving to Ipswich and she was looking for someone to replace her present job as a 'nanny-share'. Parents of both families worked full-time, so the idea of having one nanny sharing responsibility for their little ones and splitting the cost was working for all parties involved. The initial start date for the role was in September, which was just perfect.

My former family in Earlsfield invited me to spend their annual holidays in Cornwall at the end of August before my new job started. It was my first time in this part of England and I fell in love with it at first sight. I couldn't get enough of gazing at the sun from atop a cliff overlooking the sea and the deep, dark sky with thousands of stars twinkling at night. My soul felt at home being reconnected with the natural beauty of it all. It gave me the strength for new beginnings. This was also around the time when I met the psychic. It seems that whenever I spend time in nature it brings more clarity to my path.

# 7. Transition Time

Now, the psychic said that I shouldn't worry about men. After the soldier disappeared from the scene, I fell under the spell of five men whose first name started with a letter 'J'. 'J' No. 1 entered my life during my study years and he broke my heart. Funnily enough, they all worked in finance. The number five also played a role. I was born on the fifth. I had to work for five English families before I broke the chain. In my life I also have five close female friends with the name Cristina, either spelled with a 'C' or a 'K'. I think there is something peculiar about names and numbers in my life. But the lovers' names starting with the letter 'J' working in the world of finance felt like the Universe was having a laugh! This pattern kept reappearing until I realised that the rollercoaster with the financial J's wasn't going to nourish my soul. It was 'J' number five whose words stood out when he said: "I forgot how deep you are!" In that instant he hit the nail on the head. I was simply too thoughtful, and my colourful mind clashed against the black and white numbers set in stone within a numerical mind. It became so evident and clear after he said this that I never questioned or worried about the financial J's of the past ever again. You can call me naive or innocent or pure, but I do believe in true love, and I'd rather spend the rest of my life alone than sharing it with the wrong person.

Forget about men for now, I told myself. With my enrolment on the course in October 2006, new challenges were to be faced! One of them, and the most important one, was, ironically, the finance. The man with psychic abilities advised me that I shouldn't worry about those; he said the money would come. I couldn't possibly ask my parents for help. They'd always supported my journey and the advice I was given was to follow my instincts. They had given me unconditional love and the freedom to do as I pleased. That was the greatest gift for me. I assume the greatest gift I have given them back is that I've supported myself financially since I left my country at the age of nineteen.

And then a helping hand came out of nowhere. I'd kept in touch with the family in Earlsfield, those I'd lived with as an au pair before I'd moved out to work as a nanny. After I told them about my study plans they offered for me to come back to live with them when I started attending university. I was to help them with childcare in return for accommodation and food while I went to study. Everything started to fall into place.

I remember one train commute after a day's work from Clapham Junction to Streatham Common. It was during mad April weather just after a storm. The clouds were clearing as we were passing Balham and all of a sudden the bright rays of the sun penetrated through them. It felt like I was seeing the most beautiful sunset in the UK since my arrival. A new world of possibilities was opening up. I felt so alive and I felt excited again as new doors were opening up for me. I had faith that the Universe was on my side!

But then suddenly I started to feel let down by my thoughts once again. The idea of having to return to old ways of living with a family and losing my independence felt sad. The thought of going back wasn't appealing. But I also knew it was necessary in order for me to survive, so it had to be. Sometimes we have to take a step back in life in order to move forward – this was the thought I comforted myself with. The purpose of it all was to accelerate the pace moving from one profession to another, from being someone who looks after other people's kids to move into a field that interested me and to get into the industry once my degree was finished. I had to suffer the discomfort of losing my independence once more so I could progress further. My focus was on the studying and looking out for the light at the end of the tunnel. There was no other way forward.

During this time I had a very vivid dream. It put shivers down my spine when I read this stuff in my diary, as I had completely forgotten all about it…

*I saw myself in the family home of the parents who offered me their room. The mother and I were having a friendly conversation at the end of the day, while the little girl I used to look after was sitting at the table in the kitchen. It felt like I was already enrolled in the course as a student. Then a doorbell rang. The mother went to see who it was and said I had a visitor who wanted to talk to me. Who could this be? I thought to myself… I wasn't expecting anyone. I walked to the front door and there was a professor from my former fashion school from Slovakia. He told me not to live with the family. He didn't say the reason why, only that it wasn't suitable for me to live there…*

My former professor died in an accident a few years back when I was still studying in my own country. A lorry crashed into him while he was riding a bicycle on the road. He was in his mid-thirties, had a wife and two children. They announced it while we were sitting in a class waiting for him to turn up. Only that he never did… We were left speechless. My dream felt like a premonition. I felt very confused when I rediscovered this in my diary, hence the reason I wrote it down. Was this a clear message? Was I not supposed to abandon my freedom and pull through some other way? How? That was the question! How was I to manage without their support? I thought the family's offer for helping me out with accommodation while studying was a crystal-clear message from the Universe that they were there to support me! Where did this man come from to tell me otherwise? It was a couple of years since he'd died and we never even had a chat when he was alive! It was a mystery. My mind was muddled up, big time. How was this possible? The Universe was sending me such confusing messages. I pushed the dream to one side and ignored it. I wasn't ready to fight again. Not again. I didn't want to put myself at a risk of not being able to finish my degree by being thrown out on the street. How would that have worked otherwise? I couldn't see it clearly. I couldn't put my future at stake by losing this opportunity to progress further! How would I be able to make a living in one of the most expensive cities in the world and study at the same time with nobody's help? I knew that studying and looking after children would require great effort and hard work, but I also knew that I could make it that way. I didn't know how else I was supposed to make it happen otherwise. Was I not supposed to be safe?

Today I know there is always a way. The Universe would have had my back and perhaps conspired to find a different route for me. That was the message of my former professor – there were ways for me not to lose my freedom and push through. However, back then I was too afraid to risk it all. At the end of the day, there are many routes in life; it depends on which one we choose. And I have chosen the one that was more comfortable, with a roof above my head, as I was too afraid to live in discomfort, especially after my earlier struggles, having to move five times as an au pair. And I didn't want to become homeless.

Towards the end of the summer came another vivid dream:

*I was with a group of students; it felt like a school trip. I was one of the students. We were by the seaside and it was pretty dark as there was a big grey cloud in the sky. The sea was open and wide and there were islands in the sea, and there was a great distance between them. Our group was led by a teacher, and the person who was in charge told us to swim through the sea to reach one of those islands. So we all jumped in, but shortly afterwards someone was eaten by a shark. There was great fear and hysteria as there were many sharks now in the sea! All of us were in the water! Everyone panicked! I was frightened for my life. I was scared that I would be the next one the shark would get. The sea was wild and dark! The students were screaming! I could feel a heavy, dark energy. Somehow I managed to swim back to the shore, and I felt enormous relief. I still couldn't believe that I'd made it! By now the person on the shore who was in charge had a register and was checking who'd survived. Then a weird thing happened... She came up to me and said: "Oh, you shouldn't be here. You were supposed to be down there!" And she pointed to the sea. I had this awful feeling of great confusion and guilt. Then this person announced that the people's names that were on the list were free to leave. I wasn't on the list! But I escaped and ran off with the others...*

I shared my dream with my former Slovakian flatmate, the one who studied psychology. Her interpretation of my dream was that it reflected my emotions towards the situation I was in. She said it was a clear indication that I'd overcome a certain obstacle in life and was now free to move on. It was an interesting thought. They say dreams are reflections of our waking lives, with the truth hiding behind. I'd never had such vivid dreams in my life before, and they felt so real that I remembered whole stories – these two dreams were fairly significant for me. And I wondered if this was as a result of me meeting the psychic and these dreams were premonitions to help me to see. It was a mystery...

# 8. Study Years at LCF

## YEAR 1

At the end of September 2006, I hired a man with a van who took me back to Earlsfield, where I'd left only a year ago. University was about to start. The course I chose was a BA Honours Degree in Fashion Design and Marketing. I thought that since I studied fashion design for four years in my native country I would add marketing to it in order to progress in this field and learn something new. I received advice from my housemate that since I'd lived in the UK for three years now, I was eligible to apply for a student loan. And I did. The psychic had been right, money did come from unexpected sources, and it certainly helped with my living costs during those years. In 2006, the tuition fees for home and EU students were only a quarter of the price they are today. In 2010, the fees tripled. The timing of my three years at university had financially worked out in my favour.

During my first term at university, I felt a little overwhelmed. There was a lot of work to be done on individual projects with strict deadlines. It was one of those 'feel the fear and do it anyway' tasks. I didn't have time to do anything else apart from learning and looking after the kids in the family I lived with. I had time to breathe while I was running.

Running was my saviour, a way of taking the events of the day and then exhaling in the evening. It became part of my everyday routine. Sooner rather than later I came to the conclusion that marketing wasn't 'my cup of tea'. Anything related to research, consumer needs and strategies I found terribly boring. On the other hand, we had very interesting lectures from people in the industry whose insights were extremely valuable. One of them that I was fond of was a lecturer of fashion forecasting. She worked for Mintel Reports, the company that carries out research in the consumer market, and she had an in-depth knowledge of what was happening in the industry. She used to say to us: "What people need and look for these days are people we can rely on!" She was beyond the age of having children and revealed that she and her partner had decided not to have any. She was a true inspiration and a living example that we're never too old to learn, as she attended evening classes at Westminster University and studied further herself. I always looked up to her for her enthusiasm to share her knowledge and desire to teach and connect with the young crowd. It worked both ways, and there was a youthfulness imprinted all over her.

Our class consisted of a real mixture of kids from every corner of the world. The majority were younger than I was, but we had a few mature students too. There were girls from South Korea, Taiwan, Japan, Estonia, Germany, France, Hungary, and even Trinidad and Tobago. We also had a group of girls from India who were all related to one another. The rest of the class was formed of native English speakers; you could count them on the fingers of one hand. I was astonished to realise that the majority of them had never used a sewing machine or held a pencil in their hand in their life. Let's say I was fairly disappointed in not having a peer to compete with when it came to the design and creative side. And I never found a real friend in my class either. The reason might have stemmed from the fact that I never had the chance to socialise with any of them outside the college due to my commitments after class. There was no time for that. I always fit in everywhere very easily, but I never truly belong. Today I know better. Today I know that the feeling of 'not belonging' was a limited perception of reality created in my own mind. It was an illusion that I fed myself in order to feed my vulnerable Inner Child. The true reason behind it all was that my situation was simply different to the other kids in the set-up of things, as most of them were financially supported by their families, while I had to do it myself.

For three years straight I spent every single weekend in Earlsfield looking after children in the daytime while their parents played golf in Sunningdale. The evening was spent studying within the four walls of my room upstairs, while they were having dinner parties in the kitchen downstairs. Despite knowing I was making progress, the university years were hard on me. Often, tears streamed down my cheeks, and I badly wanted everything to be over and done with. Despite following my dream, I felt like a bird in a cage with my wings trimmed. The call for independence was gnawing at me. I wanted to be free. Evolution doesn't happen without suffering.

All I knew to get me through this period was patience and persistence. My first year of study was slowly coming to an end. There was a design project with a focus on reinventing denim that I poured all my energy into. I created a strong portfolio of work, including a made-up outfit that I sewed myself, and I received 96 credits out of 100 in the module when it was finished.

There was a small presentation with a catwalk in our class at the end of that year, and a former creative director of Asda clothing was invited to come along and judge our creations. I didn't pay a lot of attention to this since I wasn't interested in high street chains until I won the first prize among my peers. And then my face and ears turned red from the anxiety of being seen when I had to collect my prize. I don't think I'll ever overcome my shyness of being in a spotlight. Towards the end of it, I had a brief conversation with this creative director and he said that my design stood out among the others as it had strength, in a good way. And then he asked me a question: "What do you want to do when you finish your degree?"

I simply said the first thing that entered my mind: "I just want a job, really."

And he laughed…

It was the summer of 2007, when the entire retail industry was at the height of disposable fast fashion. People were shopping for clothes the same way they shopped for food. Celebrities and designers all jumped on the wagon, accelerating the pace by creating 'limited lines' in collaboration with more affordable high street chains. Girls would buy an outfit for a Friday night out and throw it out the window the next day. Nobody was worried about the security of a job upon graduation in the midsummer of 2007, no one but me…

As a student under the umbrella of the University of the Arts, I had access to a thing called 'Blackboard'. Blackboard is an online platform where people from the industry look for young creative individuals and students for internships or voluntary work to improve their skills while studying to enhance their employability once they finish their degree. An internship for Alexander McQueen's studio was advertised there. I applied, and soon after, I was called for an interview. In the initial job description they were looking for a student who could commit for a one-month period. That was perfect considering I would have some spare time ahead before the kids broke up for their summer holidays, I thought.

I felt ecstatic beyond measure carrying my design portfolio to their studio. It was a different story when I got there. In reality, they were looking for someone who was able to commit to a minimum of three months from the start to the end of a new collection. You hear all these stories of fashion interns being exploited, working endless hours for free… I never found out myself. I told myself that it didn't matter that I didn't get in, because I'd tried.

I went back on Blackboard and found something else. There was a freelance opportunity to help to create a wardrobe for the cast in an upcoming theatre play called *Madonna and Me*. I signed up for it and agreed to meet the playwright. He was working at the *Guardian* at the time and writing plays was his passion. We met in the Starbucks near Angel station, and we discussed all that was required and I agreed to go for it despite it not being paid. I had to start somewhere to gain experience in the field so I could stick something on my CV. I would get fifty quid to help source material for the costumes and create outfits that were inspired by the eighties, as the whole play was set in that time period. Basically, the playwright was originally from Merseyside, near Liverpool, and the story was autobiographical, as he was gay and a massive Madonna fan. She inspired him to come out of his shell and travel down from the North of England to London. He must have been in his late thirties at the time, and so it was amusing looking back at how we tend to evaluate our past when we hit middle age.

I was lucky, because I was allowed backstage to watch them rehearse before the play hit the stage. What an experience! There was so much going on behind the scenes... I had no clue about... anything! How each character had to own their act, how each actor had to carry themselves, how they said things, which way they said them, when to raise their voice and how to give room to others... It was an absolutely jaw-dropping experience – I was in awe! I was utterly mesmerised, and I loved being there absorbing every minute of it. They made such an impact on me that I started blaming myself for choosing the wrong industry! The cast were struggling to get by, often working two or three different jobs simultaneously in order to feed their thirst for acting. Hats off to that! Acting, music, and I guess fashion comes after that – the toughest industries to break into!

It had a premiere at the Union Theatre in Southwark near Waterloo, and then in August the play moved to Jermyn Street Theatre in the West End.

On a few occasions the crew asked if I would join them for a drink afterwards, but I had such an incredible respect for those guys that I built that wall around me again and turned them down; I was incredibly shy. But when it came to the end of the last performance I thought it would be rude not to. I liberated my soul from the depth of my insecurity at being seen by strangers, my inhibitions and shyness crossing the boundaries of my comfort zone, and I just let go – I had a blast! It was the best night out ever! There was no one there to judge. At the end of the day we were all free creative spirits living in the present moment as the evening unfolded. We squeezed into G-A-Y club and danced the night away to the eighties hits of Madonna, Kylie and Michael Jackson, getting lost in the big screens. The crew handed me an envelope with some 'dosh' for my efforts and a thank you card, and one member of the cast, who was straight, as opposed to the rest, had left a message inside that read: "Will You Marry Me?" Hilarious! It was the sweetest thing that someone I'd got to know over a couple of fortnights had ever written to me! Then I got wasted... and I got hit on by a lesbian... and the rest I don't remember... my last memory was of me standing outside the entrance barrier climbing on top of the bars and running straight back into the club and shouting at the bouncers: "Let me back in! I was having a fag! Let me back in!" And then a voice rang in my ears – the voice of one of the crew members: "Let her in! SHE'S ONE OF US!" And I did get in – finally I'd found my crowd, if only for a night!

## YEAR 2

My second year of study carried on in the same spirit as the previous one. My focus was all about hard work and dedication to gain the best possible results in my chosen subject. However, it was at this time my soul started feeling increasingly isolated and far from nature, which had played such an important part of my upbringing. I badly yearned to run to the forest, but there wasn't one! Since I didn't have many trees to climb near Earlsfield, I turned my search inward. We all have our own shadows and fears and I decided to face them by creating my own 'journey through self-discovery'. This was a small diary where I poured all my dark thoughts and insecurities into small drawings. Throughout my studies, I suffered from a fear of failure, and by addressing my anxieties in this little sketchbook, I found a way of releasing my fear and I managed to move on, pushing myself forward.

**No. 1: Fear of failure**

**No. 2: My fear is losing its power**

**No. 3: Fear of getting a 'big hot block'… and overcoming that fear**

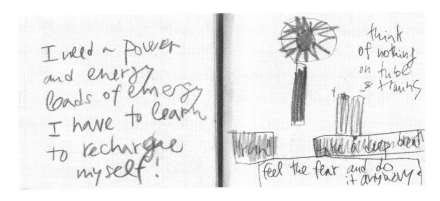

**No. 4: Draw power and energy to recharge myself**

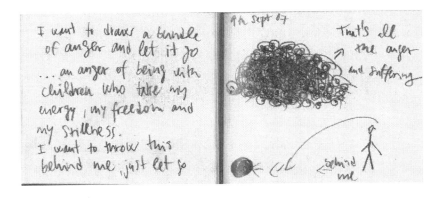

**No. 5: I want to release a bundle of anger**

At the end of the day, nothing and nobody is perfect, but everything and everybody is made in the best possible way they can be... I finished the second year of study successfully.

# YEAR 3

The beginning of my third year in autumn 2008 started off with a great disappointment. It wasn't only due to the economic downturn, which was followed by the great recession and unemployment on the rise, but I felt terribly sad because my course director announced that our major final project would be a written dissertation. From the very start, I believed that upon finishing my course I was expected to create a collection of designs and not a written piece of work. This was very problematic for me as my focus for the past three years had been taken from me. I'd wrongly assumed that creating a collection upon graduation would be the triumph of my creative soul. I thought this would allow me to take part in the LCF Graduate Fashion Week, which would then get me a foot in the door to the industry! I felt betrayed. I had a dilemma about whether I should propose a change of direction in my final year for one where they would allow me to focus on a design project. And on top of this, my tutor didn't support me at all! I shared my concerns but all she could say was that I could do both a final dissertation and create a capsule collection at the same time. "It's up to you, but nobody has ever done that before," were her exact words. I was freaking out! There would be no time to commit to both and achieve excellence. I wanted to give it my all! And splitting my time between two final projects within a time restriction for only one didn't seem like a good plan. I considered the dilemma for two weeks straight, with no one there to advise me on what to do next… so I gave in. I played it safe. My heart wanted to play but in my mind I feared that if I didn't obey the rules and produce a piece of work that was expected, I would fail. And so my final project was to write twelve thousand words of a written dissertation with a small design project on the side. If I had a regret in my life so far – that was it! Today I wonder whether if I'd listened to my heart instead of my brain and took the leap of faith, where might that have led instead!

With my final piece of writing I investigated the topic of 'When Does Fashion Become New'. They say fashion is a reflection of any given period, and it's created under the influence of the spirit of that time, called the 'zeitgeist'. For my design portfolio of creative work, I chose the life of Vincent Van Gogh and his art as my main source of inspiration. I divided his life into four major themes. It started off with an episode of black and white drawings that I called 'Experimentation with a Single Line', about an early stage of his life, followed by 'In the Mood for the Light of the Sun', based on his masterpiece called *Sunflowers*. The next chapter was called

'Self-expression', about when Van Gogh cut off his ear and made a self-portrait, and the final stage was 'In the Mood for the Eternal Night Sky', based around his famous work of art called *The Starry Night*. It is clear that Van Gogh used nature throughout his life as a driving force in his art. With my tribute to his many masterpieces, I showed how I was influenced by those episodes of his life and used them as background themes for the design and development of my own creations, inspired by his array of colourful palettes that were unique for each one. From this portfolio of creative design development, I was able to choose one to be made up.

In the early days of 2009 I played with the idea of applying for an MA in Fashion at Central St Martins. I sent off my application and this time I was called in for an interview. There were about twenty of us in the room. They only selected two students to study the MA in Womenswear in the academic year ahead. I wasn't one of them. Nevertheless, I was happy to be part of the process. Deep inside I knew that I didn't want to be a student any more, but then I didn't want to be unemployed either, and I thought holding a diploma from the most celebrated fashion institution in the world might help to gain a better entry at a prospective job a year later.

At least I'd tried, though I failed again. My main focus was now clear: to enter the world of uncertainty and move out to find a place of my own before the kids broke up for the summer holidays. The job search was on.

While I was occupied with working on my final dissertation, as well as making up my final design project, I applied for internships. On the 21st of April 2009, I had a trial day at a studio for a possible three months' work experience. On the 22nd of April, a sudden phone call put everything at a standstill. My plan had been to visit home in May that year after the submission of my projects, but death doesn't work according to a fashion calendar or a deadline in the schedule. Life simply comes and goes.

I was sitting behind a sewing machine in the famous LCF campus site on Curtain Road near Old Street, finishing my design project, when my sister rang. She called me only twice while I was in England. The first occasion was to tell me of the death of my granddad and the second was the birth of her firstborn son. I ran into the corridor as I couldn't hear her because of the noisy machines. Her voice echoed in my ear: "Granddad has died."

I leaned against the wall and tears welled up in my eyes as a gentle caress of shivers ran down my spine. I couldn't miss it – an inner voice reminded me of the promise I'd made some time ago – I had to be at the funeral.

My sister's voice brought me back: "Are you there? Andrea?"

I was lost for words. With a shaky voice, I asked: "Do you know when the funeral is?"

"I don't know yet. I only just found out that he's passed away and wanted to let you know," she said.

I was never more grateful to my sister in my entire life that she'd broken the news at that time. Later that afternoon I called my mum and asked her if she knew when the funeral was. She didn't. My mother tried to reassure me that it would take a couple of days to arrange. I wasn't convinced. I asked her to go next door to my aunt's house and find out while I was waiting on the line. My auntie was triumphant again! She managed to organise the funeral in two days, no questions asked. No need to wonder 'why'. It shouldn't have been a surprise by now. I had to act fast. That day was Wednesday. I flew home on Thursday evening. The funeral ceremony was held on Friday at noon. He had been ninety-four years old.

When it was over and done with, I went to see my family next door. My aunt told me the priest who gave her father the last farewell had never seen a man so ready and happy to leave this world behind as granddad was when he left this life. My aunt was in the opposite state of mind as tears trickled down her face in the garden where we were sitting. There were just the two of us sitting side by side. And then she made a confession I didn't understand. She begged him for forgiveness before he took his last breath. I was puzzled by her revelation, and a thought crossed my mind: if you live your life with dignity and truth, you have nothing to be ashamed of or to hide from or to be forgiven for in this life; isn't that right? I wasn't strong enough to tell her that at the time. It could have been perceived as cruel to mix this into the feelings that occupied her at this time. I was wondering what to say to offer some kind of comfort or solace and this is what came out.

"Well, I'm convinced granddad is looking down on all of us now."

She stopped crying and looked me up and down in disbelief, as if I'd fallen from another galaxy. I was unsure what she was thinking. My aunt was the first in the church every single Sunday morning, yet she didn't believe in the afterlife.

My granddad was an interesting man. I wish I'd spent more time with him while he was alive. He was born on the 13th of December in 1915. His dad was killed in the First World War when he was only one year old. My granddad fought in the Second World War. He was a partisan hiding in the mountains. Slovak partisans were formed during the national upheaval in 1939 to fight against the Nazis. All my granddad ever talked about was how he used to run from one mountain to another for weeks on end without any food supplies. The last time I saw him he told me that once he and his comrades were passing a small cottage in the middle of a forest somewhere in Poland, and a woman that saw them left a small cup of fresh warm milk straight from a cow outside her house on a windowsill. She must have known they were hungry and left the milk there for them to share while she hid inside the house hoping not to be seen. I wish I knew more stories of what he got up to during the war. However, a wise man once told me that he himself probably didn't know which direction they were going in as they were running from one place to another. My granddad only had one good eye. He got shot during the war so one of his eyes was made of glass. Two or three years before he passed away, I painted a portrait of him and tried to capture his essence from this photograph I kept. On one of my visits back home I took it to him and was totally amazed to find him reading newspapers without a magnifying glass! I showed him my artwork and asked him directly: "Granddad, tell me, who is this man in the picture?"

In the old local dialect of a village man, he replied: "Would it be me?" And he laughed. It was the best moment we shared together, that last time. And I locked that treasured moment into my heart; it's forever mine.

**My Grandad's Portrait**

# 9. One Foot in the Door

So there I was, a fresh graduate, and I'd managed to get a foot into the industry, in the midst of a double-dip recession. I joined a company as a fashion intern on the 5th of May 2009 and was to stay for three months. The womenswear line had launched less than a year earlier in September 2008, and its original very small team consisted of dedicated young professionals. I must have done something right, I thought, when I got in the door. With my curiosity and observant nature, I tried to digest everything that was happening and I was thrilled to be part of it. From the beginning, I couldn't believe my luck and often had to pinch myself in order to believe it.

There was great tension one morning in the office. There was a fitting in progress with a French couturier at the scene and I had to step in as the other member of staff who was supposed to be in the meeting got held up on the Tube during the morning commute. Luckily for me, I was asked to replace him and take photographs throughout the session where necessary. It was immensely interesting to be present and to watch until the delayed member of staff appeared and I had to leave. Still, there was plenty for me to absorb all day long.

My major responsibility was to support the production manager, but I was also put in charge of creating design illustrations that were used for spec sheets, or flat drawings as they are called, and those illustrations also appeared in sales books for public relations. I was lucky as they required drawing by hand at that time; I am one of those old-style designers who prefer hand sketching as opposed to using Illustrator software.

There were amusing moments too, like when I was given a task to get Flowerbomb in forty-five minutes one sunny day; the perfume by Viktor and Rolf is the bomb we are talking about. This was a personal favourite of an 'LA' stylist who was visiting the studio and was about to leave. I was lucky! The Peter Jones department store in Sloane Square was easy to get to. The only problem I had to face was the traffic. Nevertheless, I did it in less than half the given time and giggled all the way back as I felt like the character of 'Andrea' or 'Andy' played by Anne Hathaway in the movie *The Devil Wears Prada*! Fashion does contain a funny bunch of people!

One day I was approached by a member of the team to ask if I would be willing to help out during a photo shoot that coming Saturday, but I was too bloody loyal to the family whose kids I looked after every single weekend and said 'No'. My head went into overdrive as soon as I realised the mistake I made. Those chances are rare! After about twenty minutes I went back to say I'd changed my mind, but it was too late! The spot had already been taken. Fashion doesn't wait for anyone – take it or leave it! Those who wait, lose. I said no while the Universe was offering me this chance on a plate. I felt trapped in life and I didn't listen once again. I think the fact that I am a dog in the Chinese zodiac didn't help either... I was afraid of letting other people down and I let myself down instead! I wish I'd known what Richard Branson would have said: "If someone offers you an amazing opportunity and you are not sure you can do it, say YES – then learn how to do it later."

***

My results from the final year arrived. My course director informed me that had I not forgotten to include a 'rationale' upon handing in my piece of design work I would have gained first class honours. At the end of the day it's only a grade – it's the journey that matters. My mission to gain a BA degree was slowly coming to an end. The graduation ceremony was held on the 14th of July 2009 in the Central Hall, Westminster. I hadn't invited my parents to the ceremony because I had nowhere for them to stay, and secondly, I didn't want them to go through the pressure of taking a flight. My parents have never taken an aeroplane in their entire life. My course director was intrigued, as most of the students had their relatives present at the ceremony. My explanation of their absence took her by surprise when I replied that I didn't think it to be such an achievement, but I was in denial to myself. I knew they would have been incredibly proud; there was no question of that. But I also knew that for my parents it would have been better news if their daughter had secured a job instead and had both feet in the industry as opposed to having just one in the door! I gave myself a month to move out from the family I lived with and find a paid job.

Just a week after the ceremony a friend of a friend announced that there was a small room up for a rent in Southfields. I took it straight away as I didn't want to lose the opportunity, and I moved from the family in Earlsfield the following weekend. They were very supportive and understanding, as always. It was a three-bedroom flat in a dodgy part of Southfields and I was to share with two Slovakian couples, but the highlight was that Wimbledon Common was only ten minutes away. Here, I found solitude among the trees and a new area for a run to escape the city.

Since my internship was due to reach the end of its three months' period, I had to come up with a plan and make the internship work alongside a part-time job. It was going well and I didn't want to lose it. I found a recruitment agency who offered temporary retail jobs in Selfridge's department store, though I wasn't impressed by the idea of waiting each morning to see if I would be called in or not. In the meantime, I looked elsewhere. Most of all I hated the idea of wearing a black uniform and court heels; it scared the hell out of me! Uniforms and I do not mix well. I was called in for a trial day and they gave me a 'yellow' branded badge with my name on it. However, in sympathy to my hatred for uniforms, the Universe once again heard my call. That same day, I was offered a part-time job in a small luxury swimwear boutique in the heart of Chelsea and I never had to wear the black uniform with the branded Selfridges badge at all! Deep sigh of relief!

The first three months of my internship were full of excitement as every day there was something new to learn. After the three-month period, I proposed the idea of working for two days a week. The management agreed and kept me on the books; they understood that I had to earn a living in another job. For the first three months of my internship I thrived, but in the second stage of my time there something changed. I had an enormous feeling of isolation, although I was still part of the team. It was that feeling of not truly fitting into the tribe again, being an alien, an outsider who felt misunderstood and a little weird. I yearned for a connection, for someone to understand me.

At this stage they allowed me to work with pattern cutters and use a sewing machine too, and it felt good to be part of the creative process. Yet something was up; I could feel it in the air. They kept bringing in new interns who could afford to work full-time. I watched all the other English interns and how they interacted with the senior members of staff and I kept thinking that I wished I could be part of the gang, but the reality was *I was different*! I was an outsider once again, and I wished and longed for true friends and for a relationship that I'd never known, for someone who truly understood me, for someone who was a real friend!

And then it happened. After six months, they asked me to leave. The reason? Well, human resources announced that part-time interns could be replaced by those who are able to work full-time. Again, the privileged kids would get the job! I had to earn a living elsewhere in order to work a few days for free while little rich kids were able to work full-time while the parents paid the bills! It didn't matter how talented, eager to learn, driven or determined to succeed you were. Money rules the world! No exceptions! And if you don't have that financial support, you may as well go and blow!

The day they broke the news was a memorable one. I was called in to have a meeting in the afternoon in a freshly decorated room where new mirrors were fixed to the back wall. The two team leaders who had initially offered me the internship made the announcement. I felt torn to pieces. Straight away I told them how sad I was. I told them that it felt as if there were more of us in the

65

room; it felt like that because of the reflection in the mirror. I knew it would come to an end sooner or later but I had no clue it would finish all at once just like that. I had a flashback to the moment when I was hired for the role and thought to myself how naive I'd been hoping there was a chance to progress and become a member of staff that would eventually be paid if I proved myself worthy. And I ignored the ironic smirk in the corner of their mouths as I was terribly naive in thinking that I had a chance. Now the hopes I'd had were falling apart like a house of cards.

On another note, my time there was framed by two major family incidents: the passing of my granddad and the birth of my sister's firstborn son at the end of it. I was now free to go and see him for the first time. I became a godmother. There is an old saying that when a member of a family dies another will be born soon... and so it was.

# 10. Friendships for Life

W

They say when one door is closing another will open up soon. To my surprise, the new door was almost waiting for my discovery, and I'll never forget how it came about. The day I was told that my internship was coming to an end I researched on Blackboard once again. This was the same online resource through the London College of Fashion where my previous internship was found. There it was in black and white – a young British fashion designer was looking for a studio assistant to help with the day-to-day running of a high-end womenswear brand. Strangely enough, his name came during my internship. The management team talked about this young British talent and how extraordinary it was that he did everything himself.

The day after that, I couldn't access Blackboard any more because my login details expired – a new academic year was about to start. But then I remembered that I'd written the designer's email address somewhere on a piece of paper and found it in the trash bin late at night. Hooray! I wrote him an email straight away. It was a question of life and death. Somehow, I was aware that the experience I would gain from this opportunity would give me much more than I knew at the time. I felt a kind of mysterious pull towards the designer. He responded immediately.

It was a cold Saturday morning early in November 2009 when I went to meet him for the very first time. I carried a large portfolio of work in one hand and a big umbrella in the other, hiding from the rain and fighting with the wind. In contrast to that, the minute I stepped through his door, a feeling of calm and tranquillity washed over me. W came across as the most down to earth human being I have ever had the pleasure to meet, especially in London. I spied a tiny little studio with a work table and a sewing machine and I couldn't help wondering how on earth did he manage to complete a collection in this place! Wow! What a contrast to the studio premises I'd just left. As our conversation progressed, my admiration for this young designer grew – all I can remember was that I didn't want to leave. There was an instant connection, as if we'd met before. The friendship I'd never had, the one I was craving for, the one I was thinking about and never thought was possible had suddenly appeared in front of me! It felt as if the two of us had been predestined to meet, written in the stars...

What twist of fate had brought me here? Had the Universe once again conspired in my favour and heard my call for a close friend? It's a mystery.

W's personal life had possibly played a significant role in why I felt such a strong connection to his persona. His story touched me deeply. I admired that he'd remained strong despite everything he had been through in life, and I felt terribly fond of him. He never knew his dad, as he'd left his mother when he was three and his mother had died when he was only eighteen years old, and that was the time he moved to the capital to study fashion at LCF. Upon graduation, he went to work for a French couture house in Paris. In the meantime, an Italian fashion house had selected the designer's first collection when he was a runner-up in the Fashion Fringe competition for emerging new talent during London Fashion Week, and from there W went off to create his own label with the help of his former boyfriend.

My daily routine now consisted of a part-time job in a swimwear shop in Chelsea, but I lived for those two days working for his brand. Through W I met my best friend, AKS, who also worked as his assistant in the studio. She'd graduated from Kingston University with a degree in fashion design and we clicked from day one. Finally, I felt I truly belonged; it was here that I met my kind of people, my tribe. I was poor and yet so fortunate! Those were the happiest days of my life!

Soon the studio moved from this little room to larger premises on the top floor of a building that had huge windows overlooking The Shard, which was just being built. Here in the studio, AKS and I would often jump up and down from the sheer joy and thrill of it all. There was the excitement of being alive and working in the industry, although it was still for free. I knew it wouldn't last forever but I couldn't care less because it was all about living in the present moment. There was an ambience of magic in the air, where anything was possible. We helped to create W's designs and were part of all that was happening behind the scenes.

As the year came to a close I couldn't help thinking that 2009 had turned out to be anything but boring. Life was progressing in the most peculiar way. In summary, I gained my BA degree, moved out, found a retail job, lost my granddad and became a godmother, worked for a well-known celebrity and perhaps lost the opportunity of a lifetime, but I gained more, much more! I gained a friendship for a lifetime meeting my soulmate and best friend AKS, plus J No. 3 was also on the scene. Life is funny, sometimes…

In February 2010 we showed W's brand new autumn/winter 2010 capsule collection at London Fashion Week. We were thrilled to be working backstage amongthe madness of it all. During this period W was approached to create an art installation in Queen Victoria's bedroom for the Enchanted Palace Exhibition at Kensington Palace, and at the same time collaborations with celebrities were pouring in from every possible direction and we were all part of it, going to premieres and parties, being behind the scenes, rubbing shoulders with some of the greatest talents in the fashion industry.

And then W, his partner and I were off to New York to show the spring/summer 2011 collection in the Big Apple. I was the only one invited as AKS couldn't get her visa in time. New York had always been on my bucket list, and out of the blue this was to become a reality in September 2010. Yaaaay! I couldn't quite grasp the fact that it was true! I still recall the smell of candyfloss that lingered in the air once we'd landed at JFK. The amusing part of it is that I lived in a suite in the Waldorf Astoria on Park Avenue and saw the city streets mostly from the windows of this iconic building. The week was full-on, as we worked day and night ahead of Fashion Week. When we finally managed to get things done, which was often in the wee hours, I couldn't sleep – my bedroom was a dressing room between the master bedroom and a beautifully decorated bathroom in art deco style. So there I lay with my eyes wide open and my mind racing and going wild night after night; my insomniac-self kept me awake.

One evening I managed to sneak out to see my former college friend from Slovakia. Seven years had passed since we'd last seen each other and gone our separate ways, fleeing to different continents. That night we climbed to the top of the Empire State Building while chatting. It felt like it was only yesterday when we'd parted.

Towards the end of NY Fashion Week, there was a party. It was aimed at the Brits that were in the Big Apple, to celebrate the end of it together. More socialites and celebrities were there alongside the titled fashion crowd and important somebodies. I found myself in the whirlwind of a social hurricane and desperately needed to be away from it!

At the end of a hopeless attempt to save myself, a bald man with a shiny head stumbled across me and said: "Who do you work for?"

To which I responded: "I work as a design assistant for 'W' womenswear line. What do you do?"

"I'm a lawyer," he said... and then he added, "So, you're an intern?"

He brought me down to Planet Earth and made me feel like a nobody just to make him feel like a somebody. Oh well, there I go again, wanting to run and hide behind non-existent trees, and instead I was desperately trying to find W – he was my tower of strength. Suddenly, in among the jungle of the crowd and the dim light of the night-time, my eyes met his and we simultaneously shouted out loud: "I WANT TO SIT NEXT TO YOU!" And so we did.

Back in my early to mid-twenties, I used to party hard. Now, at twenty-seven, those days were truly over, plus I didn't feel the need to reveal my party self. I can be rather shy and an introvert around pretentious people wearing masks. Networking isn't my strength. But, I survived until the end. On the last day of the trip, I decided to walk alone from the hotel all the way to Times Square and back. The long, wide streets of New York and the tall buildings felt gigantic in comparison to the narrow streets of London's West End.

During this period, and the whirlwind of it all, W and I got to know each other more and more. Through these shared times and experiences, we created memories that would last a lifetime. The friendship I so desired had become a reality. But there was something more that had blown my mind. I questioned deeply how another soul could be so similar to my own. He would say the things I was thinking and think the things I was about to say. We were so similar, yet different, but when we were together I felt a total harmony between us. But this led to major confusion. Yes, I had fallen for W big time! This caused so much havoc in my heart – and I couldn't tell anyone. It was pure joy and sadness at the same time! I asked God why he would send someone so incredibly perfect, knowing this could never lead anywhere. My heart and soul couldn't grasp the concept that a spiritual connection doesn't take notice of the sexes. The souls of men and women are equal; the orientation of gender is insignificant.

The concept of a soulmate had never crossed my path until now. My friend Lauren Love beautifully captured the essence of what it means to meet that special someone here:

We know we know that beautiful soul, but how do we know?
We feel an inner nudge of deep resonance; soulful tingling in the heart. The familiarity in their eyes, the remembrance beneath their voice; the way their heart meets ours in synchronistic harmony. We sense ancient stories already woven, beyond our present connection so much lies beneath

the scenes. Times once past echoing within our hearts, acting as a pointer to the knowing we have deep within. Our connection sparks a memory, a harmonic resonance with our true nature. We can't hide from who we are in the presence of a soul mate, for they see who we truly are behind the veils of illusion and the layers of masks we choose to wear.

They know who we are and we know they know.

Ancient. Deep. Mystical. And oh so loving. They are here to love, guide and support us on our journey, acting as a compass keeping us on our chosen soul path. They are our divine helpers, family and soul tribe. Although they may not always serve us in the way we would like, sometimes their role is to dismantle our ego and trigger us to the core until there's just no hiding any more. You have no choice but to be true, to unravel the real you, and it is there that they shall meet you.

Once back in London I set my mind to one thing. As amazing as it felt to be involved in it all, I had to ask W to be paid for my contribution and my time spent working for the brand. It wasn't easy to do. I knew it could go either way and I feared it would risk our friendship. That fear was unfounded, but at the end of September 2010, my time at W brand came to an end. Despite all of the collaborations we did, the company didn't generate enough income to support us all. Towards the end of that year, Rihanna appeared on *The X Factor* singing 'The Only Girl in the World' wearing a showpiece that had been created for W's presentation in NYC. I didn't know about it in advance, so it was a pleasant surprise. And at that moment I felt proud that I was able to put down a marker and be part of the current zeitgeist.

## AKS

From day one, AKS and I became inseparable, not only in the studio but also in our private lives. She became my best friend, the one I would talk to about anything and everything in life. We spent our free time exploring London, having days visiting galleries, art exhibitions and going to movies, but also partying hard on Saturday nights! She was my kind of girl, full of laughter and happiness, shining brightly wherever she went. It was a joy to spend time with her and make wonderful memories celebrating life along the way.

There was one incident that stands out. It was on Guy Fawkes Night in 2010, a year after we'd met. We were heading out to celebrate Bonfire Night near Notting Hill in some primary school backyard; W and his friend were also coming. It was pretty muddy as it had rained all day and the schoolyard was very slippery. We walked behind a crowd towards the fire to meet the guys, and it was dark. Suddenly, a tall man in front of us slipped off the path and slid in the mud, falling heavily to the ground. AKS moved straight as an arrow and within the blink of an eye, offering this man her shoulder to lean on, asking if he was all right. He was twice her size. I stood there speechless... not only at how quick her reactions had been, but most of all at how kind she was! In that moment, I knew she had a beautiful heart and I had a friend for life.

AKS had a vision. She knew that one day she would have a brand of her own and so she started playing with the idea of leaving London to start pursuing her dream in Ghana, her native country. She didn't leave quietly, but with a BANG! When the Olympic Games were approaching in 2012, AKS signed up to become a volunteer to help make it all happen. Around 240,000 volunteers applied for the event and 70,000 people were chosen to be part of it. AKS was one of them; she joined the Paralympics and helped behind the scenes throughout the event. I'm a strong believer that if you give something without expecting anything in return, with a pure intention and a desire to help your fellow man, life gives back, and I'm convinced that her brand AAKS, which she was about to launch in her native country, was a blessing in advance. She set forth on her path, having a clear vision of creating a sustainable brand of beautiful handcrafted raffia bags in the most exuberant and iconic colours and prints of Africa and she's never looked back.

I have a friend called AKS. AKS is short for Akosua. It means that she was born on Sunday, like every other girl in Ghana that was born on this day. But my friend isn't an ordinary girl from Ghana, simply because she's an extraordinary girl that lives her dream, and I am proud to announce that she is my F R I E N D.

# 11. Time of Frozen Land

After my internships were truly over, I was back to square one, and I took on the role of a full-time supervisor in the same luxury swimwear shop where I was already employed. It was tough, because I'd recognised what my true passion was and worked hard to achieve where I wanted to be – yet I wasn't there! I had to try harder! The following year I was to turn twenty-eight. I had no boyfriend and no proper job in the field that interested me and that I'd been fighting for almost my whole life. I needed to take this as far as I could before it was too late and try everything I could to get there. I was also thinking that perhaps I might need to leave London, because I hadn't managed to flourish with my talent there just yet. Existential thoughts arose and ate me alive. I'd lived there for seven years now and life didn't feel very exciting any more. Throughout the summer that had just passed, I remembered some intense dreams that kept coming back to haunt me...

**First Dream:** I was in a foreign country. It was a hot sunny day and I was waiting for a train. The platform was very long. Once the train arrived I managed to load my luggage onto the carriage, but when I was about to get on board, the door of the train suddenly shut... and it left without me. I was standing there in the middle of nowhere left alone with nothing... all my things were gone...

**Second Dream:** I'd just moved into a new room or a flat where I brought all my stuff. Then, after moving in, I went out for a little walk to explore or have a bite to eat. When I returned the room had been broken into... Nothing was there. All my possession were gone… I'd been robbed, left alone again with nothing…

**Notes from my diary, 3rd Oct 2010**

> I know this might sound weird, but I think this is a sign that I have to go on a journey, look after myself and overcome the fear that something bad will happen to me in a foreign country. And I feel this is a very strong sign of embracing the unknown once again, undertaking this journey as a new path of self-discovery that will make me stronger in return. This might sound even weirder what I am going to write, but the things in those dreams have already happened to me! I feel it. And I don't think they were just coincidences, I think this journey of my life is being controlled and navigated by the Universe…

On one of those cold and crisp November mornings, I went to work not realising it was my day off. Instead of going home I went to Leicester Square. There was a shop there that I'd wanted to visit for some time containing lots of spiritual books. As I walked by, I noticed a sign in the window for palm and tarot reading. I went in and booked a session. It was freezing outside. The cold breeze was still lingering in the air as I stepped into a little space with a table behind a curtain by the front window, and I felt nervous at first. But once the man with a turban started examining my right palm, each little line carefully one by one, a wave of warmth passed through me. In an instant, I knew I was in safe hands. At his request I gave him my date of birth.

He said I'm very lucky because I don't live my life the way many people do; like my parents, for example, who have lived in the same place all their lives. He said I might live in four or five different countries and get married more than once. In fact, he asked if I'd divorced twice already… Hmmm, not that I know of.

The next question he asked was whether I'd finished my studies already, and I said I had. But I told him I wasn't working in an area that interested me yet. He said work is good, and added: "It doesn't matter what we are doing, as long as we are learning along the way." He then asked why I'd come to see him, and I mentioned a recent job interview with a company in China that I'd applied for. He said: "Don't make any long-term decisions until the 9th of January next year, four days after your birthday..." Further, he added: "If you are planning to go abroad you should look carefully into the company, because you might find yourself being trapped, or becoming somebody's slave in a foreign country." There was a card showing 'Cleopatra' being trapped in something... And then another card revealed itself, and this one was meant to indicate the present moment... it was a card showing a 'frozen land'. He said that, currently, I was in a time zone where not much would be happening for me. And then the 'horseplay' card came up. This one indicated that I could indulge sexually but I should stay protected at all times because I could become pregnant just like that. J No. 3 was a horse in the Chinese zodiac. The man with the beard, on the other hand, said that I shouldn't have children for seven to ten years. One more revelation was made; in addition to my employment, he said: "You would make a good teacher. Whatever you do, always use your creativity to your full potential." And his final advice was: "You should read Osho. His teachings would give you clarity." The end.

*** 

Back to reality. The time spent on the shop floor had become a battlefield of raw emotions; observing my own thought processes, I started having full-on conversations with the chatterbox inside my head screaming for help. On the outside, I was a shell that smiled. On the inside... oh my... On the inside I knew I could do so much better than being a shop-floor girl. This was the place to observe my anger and learn to turn my negative thoughts into positive ones. I was the alchemist who felt the pain and had to transfer it into something else. How is this done? Firstly, you become aware of your own thought processes. As soon as I noticed anger creeping in, I paused, became aware of it and observed it happening. Once a new client walked through the door, regardless of my state of mind, I approached them with a smile and forced myself to stay as positive and helpful as I could, despite my own grumpiness. Apart from a few exceptions, I've found that people with money aren't the most pleasant ones. I don't know how, but to my great surprise this technique worked wonders. Once my positive energy rubbed off on the client, we created a harmonious relationship where I would find the perfect product to match their needs almost effortlessly. This required my full presence and the gift of listening – one of the qualities I pride myself with. The shop floor became the territory where I would test the waters, and this also contributed towards my growth.

This was a period when I was reading a lot of self-help books, with guides on how to heal my energetic field, and I discovered *The Alchemist* by Paolo Coelho. I was able to put this energy work into practice. I realised that we are responsible for our own happiness, and although it was hard work, I started seeing some progress in my environment.

Imagine you are in a dark room with your fear of darkness, your anxieties and all the anger there is, but you know there's a light switch. The minute you become aware of the frustrations, turn the light on and the darkness evaporates! It sounds so simple, yet it requires a lot of patience and hard work and it doesn't happen overnight. It's a process of becoming aware of your inner workings; it's a process of becoming the master of your own energy. And once you master this task, you become lighter and more joyous in everyday life as you start discovering the lightworker within. The mind is an incredibly powerful tool… that's what I was finding out!

On one occasion, in the last hour before closing time, my manager and I were alone, with no clients in the shop. This was a late evening in November, the last day before the end of the month, and we were £600 away from hitting the target. I told my manager the following: "All we need now is for one client to walk through that door and buy two Eres swimwear costumes on the spot." Soon after that, twenty minutes before closing time, on the dot, a woman walked in to buy two Eres pieces at £300 each, and we hit the target just like that... Eres is a luxurious swimwear label, one of the best on the market.

**Notes from my diary, 1st May 2011**

Sometimes I feel truly blessed and sometimes not at all. There are little things in life, like coincidences or small miracles, that make you wonder how it's possible they happened, and then there are things that you badly want to happen or you expect things to get better and you feel like nothing is happening at all. Life is like the swing of a pendulum: one day full of joy and the next full of sadness. It's odd how it operates.

The most debilitating thing for a living human being is to lose faith. And yet I'm doing it. I've tried to apply for numerous jobs in fashion and failed again. I wonder what went wrong? Have I been cruel to someone? Is this some sort of punishment? Why can't I move forward? Is this a debt I'm paying from a past life? I keep asking myself all of these questions to no avail. I'm suffering and I don't know how long I can bear it... Tears are flooding my eyes... Self-pity is bad for you, Andrea!

***

I had once again fallen under the spell of my negative thought processes; it's one thing to master your dark shadows within a workplace, where you test the waters on the same subject again and again – it is quite another to master your mind in every aspect of your daily life. This truly takes lifelong practice and dedication to achieve and to maintain. My present situation is clearly an era of frozen land. I was endlessly applying for jobs in the fashion industry, entering design competitions and contacting agencies, but nothing came out of it. The problem was the fact that, post-recession time in the UK, when the market was hit hard, internship wasn't regarded as work experience on the fashion map. And no one was willing to offer an intern paid work experience – it was a vicious circle with no way out! I thought my life was boring and flat. No challenges. Everyday mundane nine-to-five was the norm. My life fell into a trap, and I wasn't good at that. Even the psychic said to me that routine would kill my soul… I wasn't being creative in my daily life… I had to get out!

My love life was also on rocks. I was having feelings for W, but in the evenings I was seeing J No. 3. How was the Universe supposed to make sense out of this emotional mess? The truth is, if you can't make it clear for yourself – no one else will do it! It was a time when I listened to 'Fix You' by Coldplay and cried my eyes out once again, questioning life.

And in the shattered mind of a broken heart and a failed attempt to climb the fashion ladder I forgot about one thing… I forgot a fundamental truth: a desire to be *free* – A long-ago dream that one day I wanted to chase the rainbows and the storms and travel the big wide world. I neglected the Inner Child, whose days in the past were filled with adventure and where discovery was top of the list. The once happy Eastern European child forgot how to play and smile to make her day worthwhile. And so my former flatmate, who'd travelled to South East Asia on her own, had shown me an example of how it's done! If she could do it, so could I! I'd always wanted to travel, and when would I do it if not now? It was the perfect time! And as such, I set a goal to visit Nepal.

# 12. Who Am I in Nepal?

My first solo trip to Nepal was a very smooth one indeed. My friend on my journey through Nepal was Osho; he was guiding me. Every single detail of the itinerary was rigorously thought through. I was looked after by Raj, the director of the travel agency recommended by my flatmate, from the day I arrived in Kathmandu until the day I left. He cared for me every step of the way as if I were a member of his own family. Unfortunately, I didn't keep a diary during that trip, but I can fish in my memory for the most profound moments that made me feel alive and experiences that should never fade away.

Upon my arrival, Raj was waiting for me at the airport. I received a T-shirt with the logo of his company and a necklace of garlands as a warm welcome, a long-standing tradition for a new guest entering this sacred land. In the afternoon, resting in my small bed and breakfast, I watched a beautiful monsoon from the window overlooking the bustling narrow street – the first and last rain I encountered for the duration of my trip.

The next morning, during breakfast, I bumped into a Canadian man who was embarking on a silent pilgrimage into the mountains; he couldn't believe I was setting out on a journey of discovering Nepal on my own.

That day, Raj took me to visit the Swayambhunath Stupa, also known as the 'Monkey Temple', which sits atop a hill overlooking a panoramic view over Kathmandu Valley. On the way back, we passed the main district of the city, with its famous Durbar Square. It was a place where lots seemed to be happening, and in the sharp sunlight and dust there was a strong odour of sweat from the bulls and pigs standing on the edge of the square or mingling in the nest of tangled streets alongside beggars and people sleeping rough and market stalls selling baskets of fruit, vegetables and cockerels in cages and lots of starved-looking dogs and cats everywhere. The beeping horns from tuk-tuks, motorbikes and bicycles passing alongside beautiful architecture contrasted to lamp posts with loose wires hanging off, and it got you wondering how the electricity supply could function in this way. Yet all of the above created a picture of total madness, where everything fell into place in a kind of harmonious chaos in its own charming way. This was the first time I'd experienced a Third World country, as I explored the Nepalese capital from the back seat of a motorbike.

The following morning I went on a journey by bus to the Chitwan National Park. A taxi driver was waiting at the other end and took me to a beautiful compound housing a half circle of charming little shacks built from bamboo stalks and palm leaves standing next to one another. It was late afternoon when I got there.

The owner's son showed me around and introduced me to the slow-paced life of the locals living nearby – an instant wave of calmness came over me, and the relaxed atmosphere was magnified by the golden rays of sunshine that were setting in at the time. We passed rural villages with lots of small houses, and he explained that they were built from a mixture of clay, mud and cow's shit. Bathed in sunlight, the deep earthy terracotta hues transmitted a majestic glow upon the simplicity of it all. We reached a clearing nearby where a group of women were taking part in an evening ritual of cleansing themselves and washing their clothes on the banks of a river. Just a few metres away from them, a herd of water buffalo was taking a rest.

Back in the compound at night, I realised that the beautiful bamboo shacks had some disadvantages. It sounded like monkeys were having a rave in the dark. I could hear them munching bananas and jumping up and down on my roof all night long.

The next morning I joined an organised group of Chinese tourists to experience the Chitwan Park atop an elephant. Imagine a large group of people of Chinese origin with large cameras strapped around their necks and not knowing what silence or stillness actually means. It was 'organised' chaos. We managed to see two rhinos, and the elephants got excited and chased them for a while.

In the afternoon a local guide took me on a boat ride along a crocodile-infested river. I was a little scared. I'd never had an encounter with a crocodile before, but he put me at ease, explaining that these were 'sleepy' ones. They didn't attack. I saw a number of them sleeping lazily on the shores of the river banks.

At one point, we stopped and entered a jungle in the middle of nowhere. There was an eerie noise from the insects all around, and I imagined that at any minute a big wild cat of some kind would jump out from the bushes. It was thrilling and scary at the same time, but I came out alive.

On the way back we saw the elephants from the national park at a resting station where they spent the night. I spotted little baby elephants too; they were frolicking joyfully around the mature ones. The local guide explained: "Those are all females... you see, the males are wild and free out there in the jungle. The females wait every night for the males to come down to pay them a visit. If the male elephants don't come for a couple of nights in a row the females' eyes will be full of tears in the morning – they would cry." What a fascinating revelation that was...

In the evening the taxi driver took me to see a traditional dance and a fire show in the next village. The air was hot and sticky as we walked silently side by side. On the way back he led carrying a torch for us to see and he started telling me about the possibility of hiring a watchtower in the middle of the national park where you can stay overnight. "It gives you the best chance of spotting animals at sunrise," he explained. I told him it sounded like a great opportunity, but I had to leave the next morning so there wouldn't be time. Then he said: "Your heart is too closed off. You need to open your heart and allow love to come to you."

Wooooah! Another unexpected revelation! It's one thing a man telling you about watching animals in their natural environment, but another thing completely if a man you just met the day before tells you that your heart isn't open enough! I knew they knew I was single. Everywhere I went the first question I was asked was: "How old are you" and "Are you married?" You just become immune to these inquiries into your personal life because, as sad as it sounds, this is how people in Eastern Asian countries define people. In the West, those questions are replaced by "How old are you" and "What's your job?" This is how the world operates. People like to put you in some kind of box with a label on. So, when they see a single female travelling on her own, the radar goes off as if there's something wrong. Seriously! A romance with a Nepalese man was the last thing on my mind. I was on a different mission, an adventure to explore the country! Going back to my point, just because I'm alone doesn't mean I'm lonely! And they have no idea that my grandma is with me all the time...

That night, I was sitting on the bed in my bamboo shack watching lizards climbing up the walls. Contemplating them in silence, I wondered if there was any truth in what he'd said about my heart. But no, my heart wasn't closed. My heart was broken because I was still in love with W, and I needed time to heal the wound because straight W's were hard to find.

Suddenly a humongous spider appeared. It was larger than the palm of my hand. I had never seen such a giant monster of a spider. I called the guys in to chase it, and I can't remember if they got rid of it in the end, but I know I couldn't fall asleep again! At sunrise, I parted with the owner's son, the local guide and the taxi driver, being thankful for their wonderful introduction to the nature reserve in Chitwan.

The next stage of my journey was to embark on the Ghorepani Poon Hill trek. This is a well-known hiking trail in the Annapurna Conservation Area that can easily be completed within three to four days, depending on your fitness level. When I reached Nayapul, the base and starting point of the trek, my personal guide was already there waiting for me. He became my companion and he also carried my backpack during the trip.

He was a Gurkha. And I soon came to recognise that he was a disappointed Gurkha. Disappointed in life because his brother had made it to the British Army and he did not. He missed the opportunity not because he was weak, but because he was too short.

I came to learn that for those Nepalese men, the possibility of becoming a soldier and joining a British regiment is like winning a lottery ticket. Once they fulfil the requirements and pass a strenuous physical test, they are one step closer towards the dream of being appointed to join the British ranks through a selection process. Gurkhas who have served the British Army are allowed to settle in the UK, move their family to the West and live a more fulfilling life. Perhaps he thought of himself being less of a man not being able to join the forces. He had to settle for less and accept his fate. I felt his pain.

The hiking route was pretty steep. The pathway was made of narrow steps built from the stone and rock. There were only a handful of other tourists that we passed. We met a lot of porters on the trail who were often carrying supplies in baskets attached with a piece of cloth around their foreheads... I'd never seen such a thing before. They used donkeys for the same reason too, as there were few food supplies up in the hills.

After the first day of the trek we had to stop overnight in a very simple home with a local family that my guide knew. He'd passed this way hundreds of times, and the scenery was breathtaking.

As the sun was setting with a golden glow on the horizon, I caught an idyllic picture of three local women overlooking the terraces of rice fields, and I locked that image into my heart for years to come. And then I ventured into the rice paddies on my own. It was getting a little dark as the evening was setting in. As I stood there on the narrow path, a beautiful white horse suddenly appeared in the hazy light. It felt surreal, as if someone had sent him to me. I was afraid, wondering if he was wild and free. Would he kick me from the path on the hill I was on? I tried to surrender, making myself invisible, and I waited for the creature to pass me by. And he did... and I don't even recall when and how – perhaps the feeling of wanting to surrender into nothingness was mutual... and then I wondered – had the Universe sent a unicorn to show me that magic is real? Albert Einstein said that there are only two ways to live your life. One is as though nothing is a miracle. The other is as though everything is a miracle.

Upon my return, back in the homestay, it was dinnertime. What I saw freaked me out. My guide was stuffing rice into his mouth using nothing but his bare hands. And just like that, I robbed myself of the opportunity to taste Dal Baht – the traditional Nepalese dish. The next thing I knew I was having a shower when the electricity blew. It was simply dark, cold and I was shivering. I had to find my way back into the little room on all fours up the stairs while I was giggling.

The next morning was an early start. And it was a morning like no other, because it was the first time in my life when I'd felt an overwhelming sense of gratitude. Never before this trip had I had the chance to pause and breathe. I had to come all the way to Nepal to realise that *I* was the creator of my journey, and I was free. Surrounded by the beauty of the valleys and the peaks that unfolded before me, I felt grateful to my parents for providing me with their unconditional love and the freedom to do as I pleased. I felt grateful for having had the opportunity to study fashion in London as I'd always dreamed. I was even grateful for the retail job that enabled me to pay my way… and in this state of mind I felt happiness and joy, as I set forth, for the life I was living and the air I was breathing.

That day I must have radiated some sort of positive vibe. I was going upwards step by step, little by little, but I was always ahead of my guide. He made a comment that I was strong. There was a break before we reached the top, and a bunch of local guides were sitting down and talking. You didn't need to know the language to understand what was behind this conversation… I stood alone but I stood tall! My guide told me that he'd never guided a single woman for a walk. Well, there's always a first time, I thought. Little did I know I was protected and safe during my trek. I had a handkerchief tied around my neck. It was a gift from my lover J No. 3 before I'd embarked upon my trip. It was yellow and had little white tigers printed all over it. He was originally Korean, and in their culture a tiger is regarded as a symbol of courage, power and also a guardian that drives evil spirits away, as well as a sacred creature for good luck.

It was about midday when we reached the top. The air was crisp and cold. I climbed up a big rock and greeted the sun. To enter the town you had to go through a gate. Ghorepani was a magical place. It felt like in a fairy tale, with a handful of charming wooden houses with white framed windows and shutters and blue rooftops. We settled down in a guesthouse from where I enjoyed the views. A bunch of other tourists and their guides reached there too, and I sat among the others drinking tea, as we all rested our swollen feet by the fire and dried our socks against the heat. The lemon tea was out of this world, the most delicious my taste buds had ever had the pleasure to meet. In the afternoon I took a rest in my cosy little room. The magnificent view had drawn me in. It was a sight I would never forget; gazing through the window, with carvings above my head, the smell of the fire from downstairs, in front of me was a balm for the soul: the majestic mountain peaks. It felt like the place where heaven and eternity would meet.

And in this frail and vulnerable state of mind, the blue rooftops merged with the sky and the clouds kissed the peaks and the Earth stood still and the voice from within the book I held called out and said: "Who am I?" "Don't ask," he said. "Go inside and find out who is asking..."

In that simple phrase, 'Who am I in Nepal?' Osho, my spiritual guru, officially, yet subconsciously, planted a seed. "Once the 'I' is dropped, the answer shall reveal itself."

I began a search into the depths of my soul behind those words uttered on the windowsill. Little did I know that the real search was to go inside and deep within.

And in this blissful realisation and joyous state of mind, I walked down the stairs into a magical atmosphere. In the meantime, families from the Netherlands came along, sat at the table and sang a song. I had something to eat while watching them all with a smile on my face, grinning from ear to ear.

Outside, it was dark, and you could hear the whistling of the wind from the mountain peaks against the window. The chalet had a charm of its own; it was cosy and warm. And my eyes were burning from the warmth of the fire, taking in the happiness of the atmosphere within. It felt like God himself had entered the room. I would never forget that moment filled with contentment, full of such a magical atmosphere. It made me fall in love with life all over again.

There was a porter you couldn't miss. His face was ugly beyond aesthetic measure, adorned with a set of wonky teeth, yet it was beautiful in its own way. He had the innocence of a boy who had never grown up. But when he laughed... Oh, man! When he laughed... heaven laughed with him and the whole room lit up!

The following morning we embarked on a hike, starting at 4.30 am in the dark. The highlight of the trip was to ascend Poon Hill, which is 3,210 metres above sea level. There was a large crowd of tourists, guides and porters. When we reached the top you could still see the moon and the stars and the panoramic view of the snow-covered peaks – scenery of rare beauty that was known as the fish-tail, with Annapurna, Annapurna South, Gangapurna and Machapuchare in the distance.

As we waited for the sun to hit the peaks, I caught a sight of three people in white, blue and red anoraks, and the first thought that entered my mind was that the combination of colours reminded me of my native Slovakian flag. Once again I felt at home, happy and at peace, because it doesn't matter where on the Earth I am, as long as I feel at one with the Universe. It comes from within and calls me in.

After sunrise, we set off on the descent. Going up was hard work but going down was harder than I thought it would be. I had to watch wherever I put my feet. It was painful and amusing in equal measure as my legs wobbled like jelly. Halfway down, my guide told me about wanting to find a wife, settle down and marry. I told him I was in no hurry for that yet.

From Ghorepani village, we walked into Ghandruk, had a quick break and carried on to Nayapul, from where transport was organised to take me to Pokhara Valley. I said thank you to my guide for his time as we parted and said farewell.

My legs were sore for a few days, and it was a good place to rest. Here in Pokhara, the basic bed and breakfast I stayed in had a flat roof. Each morning I climbed to the top of the valley and caught a glimpse of Annapurna once again – the perfect way to start the day. Below, in the street, I found a good spot to eat. The man in the local café made fruit porridge with honey and hot lemon tea; just what I needed. He had his wife by his side and he took great pride in his culinary skills; you could tell from his smiling face and his rounded cheeks.

During one of those mornings, as I had my favourite dish, I almost choked at the sight walking down the street. A girl, showing no remorse, wrapped only in a skimpy towel that hid very little. She was hand in hand with a Nepalese man half her size who also only had a small towel hiding his pride and joy. I overheard her British accent and was disturbed by what I'd witnessed. What the hell! I'm not judging, that's not my thing. I just wished people had some dignity! Does the whole of Pokhara need to know what happened ten minutes ago? What kind of lady does that?

The following morning at breakfast I saw another solo female traveller sitting in my favourite spot. Jenny was Chinese, worked in marketing, and lived in Hong Kong. She pointed at the Peace Pagoda atop Ananda Hill, which was visible from where we sat, but I felt that my legs were still a little too painful for that. At the end of our breakfast together, we hired a cab. We drove to the nearest point to the top and shared our travelling stories as we climbed up.

The next thing, Jenny was telling me about the paragliding that she had in mind. In the afternoon we found an agency that organised such a trip. Jenny took the lead and negotiated the price. I wasn't good at that. It was a spontaneous decision when we made the deal. I just went with the flow. The next morning would be an early start, as that was when the paragliding adventure would begin.

What I couldn't get my head around was the fact that I was to run down a mountaintop and take off just before I hit the cliff below. My instructor reassured me that once I ran towards the edge of the mountain the air would lift my feet and I would take off with the wind. I watched other people doing it, yet I couldn't believe this was the case until I ran myself and saw it happening.

Up in the air, halfway through the flight, the paragliding

instructor above me asked: "How are you?"

"YEP!" I was holding my breath, just wondering where the hell we were going to end up, and I replied: "Am OK!" And I wish I hadn't said that. The next thing I knew I was hanging like a bat, upside down, spiralling inside out, cruising above a lake like a lunatic with my stomach in my throat unable to make a sound.

I got it. With my "YEP" and "OK", that was the green light for him to show off his Batman skills.

Finally, we were heading towards the ground, and upon landing, as my head was still spinning around, I asked: "Can I please stay here for a bit?"

"You can, but not for too long as this is the landing point!"

Ha ha, that was funny, I thought. I guess I'd lost my common sense! Of course, that was the landing point and, as such, I had to crawl away like a soldier on all fours.

\*\*\*

Part of the reason for my stay in Pokhara was to spend some time with a little girl from a local orphanage. Because it was the festive season during my stay, all the other children were away with their nearest relatives. Priti was about five or six years old at the time, and she wasn't an abandoned child as such; her mother was a cleaner. She was employed in the bed and breakfast I stayed at in Pokhara, working seven days a week from dawn to dusk. In the mornings I spent a few hours with her little daughter, who practised her English writing and reading skills. Priti was a smart and clever girl. Her face was covered with little marks and I wondered why. Once when she was very little, she'd stood too close to a stove, next to her mother's frying pan, and the burning oil marked her skin for life.

After our first morning lesson, her mother invited me for lunch in the kitchen of the orphanage where they lived. Once the meal was prepared and ready to eat, we sat on the floor cross-legged, and I felt humbled, unable to refuse such a beautiful gesture, where they had so little and were happy to share as a gift. I used cutlery while the mother and daughter used their bare hands to eat. From that day on, I ate dal bhat for the rest of my trip for both lunch and dinner and couldn't get enough of it. It taught me a lesson to taste the traditional Nepalese dishes.

After lunch, Priti sat down in a playroom where she had a small TV. There was a Bollywood style love story on a loop – singing and dancing; she was mesmerised. And I saw the little girl's eyes sparkle while she was dreaming of a Prince Charming who would one day sweep her off her feet... something that only happens in a fairy tale.

This is a message to all the young girls out there who dream about Prince Charming on a white horse promising happily ever after when they meet. Love is not sustainable! Relationships are hard work and 'happily ever after' marriages do not exist. When it comes to love, you have to first love yourself before you can love another. There's no way around it. We cannot fantasise about love proving our self-worth either. Self-worth grows from within, not from without. Do you know of any princess who was locked inside a castle serving her husband forever after and who was happy until the day she died? I don't! Riches in material form bring unhappiness, fake fortune and loneliness. Love has to be unconditional, pure and free, like a gentle dance between two souls that don't touch, or a fresh breeze that caresses your face in the wind – there has to be space between the two, some notion of being free. You do not own your partner, for he or she has their own soul to please. Don't cling onto one another, for you will kill the gentle dance or the fresh breeze. Let them sing the song of their soul, and within this freedom, the desire for divine connection will grow. And in this freedom unconditional love will emanate from you. Let the song of your hearts sing the eternal sound of the unified sacred experience called love, where giving and receiving in equal measure becomes a harmony between two souls. And when it transcends from one to another, it has the greatest staying power. This is my idea of an unconditional love so rare and so hard to find, and I shall be free until the day I find it.

As my adventure in Pokhara was coming to an end, I discovered an Osho Holistic and Wellness Centre, where I treated myself to a full body massage with the focus on balancing my energy flow and healing my chakras. My memory has left me puzzled whether I was attended to by a male or female but I know it felt heavenly. What I also know is that I was completely naked and they said my hara chakra wasn't working properly, but I was leaving the next day and had no time to fix it.

The next day I was on a bus for several hours en route to Kathmandu. Raj was there to pick me up. The day after, on the way to the airport in a cab, again with Raj and the driver in the front, as we were stuck in traffic, something crossed my mind. I'd read somewhere that Kathmandu had its own elephant. I thought I'd missed it and was a little sad. In that instant, as I sat in the back between the two seats gazing through the window, in front of me, a giant elephant crossed the traffic lights out of the blue – my wish had come true! My mission of discovering Nepal had been fulfilled – it blew my mind!

\*\*\*

Upon my return from this far-off land, W announced that he and his partner were splitting up... and I thought this might be a good time for me to reveal my bleeding heart. I knew only one thing here; I do what I feel and can't go against my heart. So I took a leap of faith and made a revelation straight to his face that I loved him more than anyone I had ever met. And to my great surprise I felt more relieved afterwards. A weight had dropped from my shoulders and I felt much lighter, despite knowing he might not feel the same way. He just confirmed what I already knew; he was definitely more gay than straight. But he also made a comment that there was a very strong connection between us, a bond that he'd never felt towards anyone else, and he added that he would love to stay in touch for the rest of our lives.

After this episode, W lived in Dubai for a while, visiting London from time to time. He also went to Thailand, where he met a shaman in the jungle who said he'd left a friend behind in the UK and that we needed time apart. I hadn't heard from him for a good six to nine months. The shaman added a remark that once this period was over and done with, we would remain friends for life. And so it has been. W now lives in the USA and we are still in touch.

We're the bridge across forever, arching above the sea, adventuring for our pleasure, living mysteries for the fun of it, choosing disasters triumphs challenges impossible odds, testing ourselves over and again, learning love and love and Love! (Bach, 1984: 247)

# 13. 30 Days, 3 Countries, 30th Birthday

Once you start travelling there's no going back. Upon my return from Nepal, I started plotting my next trip. The coming year was looking very low-key, as I was saving money ahead of my next journey. I was hungry for going back to the source of what makes my Inner Child sing – discovering places I had never seen before, where my adrenaline soared high from fear and the thrill of not knowing what lay ahead, being out there, sensing the smell of the unknown in the air. I decided to go on a journey to celebrate the day I was born in an unconventional way – thirty days across three countries on my thirtieth birthday. Strangely enough, I had always felt drawn to the Far East. I love their movies, the temples, their trees; everything seems so different, exotic and mysterious – I had to follow my inner voice and explore those lands.

I landed at Bangkok International Airport a few days ahead of New Year's Eve 2012, leaving cold Britain behind. There was a challenge straight from the start to find the hotel I'd booked in advance. Lesson one: never book a taxi in Thailand as no one will be able to find the address you're looking for. Although I was exhausted from the long-haul flight, I was still in high spirits despite having to search for the right address for over three hours with a cabbie who had enough patience to help me out. Bingo at last! The hotel I was in seemed to have a lot of local girls lounging around in reception... I wondered why? It only hit me after a while as I walked downstairs and asked for a massage. The lady at reception looked me up and down and said with a smile: "The massage is for gentlemen only, please." Yikes! I'd found myself in a Thai brothel! What a start! There was a little lake in the backyard with lots of those orange fish with white stripes… Too many fish in the sea, was the thought that crossed my mind, and I giggled inside.

That night, there was a music room next door of a different kind. One little fish had got lucky at least! I was off to fly the nest of fake love the morning after, and I had the pleasure of never having to go back!

# PART 1. MYANMAR

The next day I flew from Don Muang Airport to Yangon in Myanmar according to my plan. The intention was to visit the Shwedagon Pagoda on the day I arrived. It's 2,500 years old, a national treasure, and no visit to the 'Golden Land' would be fulfilled without experiencing the ambience of this sacred Buddhist temple at first hand. It's a mesmerising sight. I visited at night when crowds of people were gathering, paying their respects, praying, worshipping the Buddha and laying offerings. It's spread across 114 acres of land; it's almost a city in its own right, with white marble floors and hundreds of golden temples, relics and shrines. Once you visit this sacred site, it stays with you for the rest of your life.

The next move was to travel to Bagan, but there was a little hiccup in that, as I could find no available accommodation ahead of my stay. I had the latest edition of Lonely Planet at hand, but every single guesthouse and hotel listed in the book was fully occupied.

In the evening, after my visit to Shwedagon Pagoda, with a little bit of hope, I handed some dollars to the boy in the reception of my Yangon bed and breakfast to try and find a room in Bagan for the night ahead. He tried calling each hotel, but to no avail. Everywhere was fully booked. I was screwed, anxious and worried, as my transport to the destination the following day was already booked. The next day I had to make my way to the station from where the overnight bus would depart. 'What will be will be' was the mantra and the plan… I had to let the Universe take over and trust the divine.

It was a hot sunny day and the air was sticky in the small waiting room. There was a small TV attached to the wall with a handful of locals glued to the screen. I was immersed in a book by Osho, my spiritual guide. He says that you should throw yourself into life experiences and only think about the consequences afterwards. As I sat there contemplating this advice I spied a foreign couple from the corner of my eye. They were clutching the same copy of Lonely Planet as I had. My radar went into overdrive as I leapt at them with questions as they arrived. They were French, on a mission to discover Bagan, and had no place to stay overnight. I wasn't the only one.

We reached Bagan at 3 am in the middle of the night. The minute I got off the bus the local tuk-tuk drivers and horse carts started asking for the name of the hotel I was staying at, only there wasn't one. There were six of us that had nowhere to lay our heads down for the night. As well as the French couple, there was a Japanese couple too and one American guy. Apparently, he'd been sitting right behind my seat on the bus all night long, but I'd never noticed him. One driver took a leap of faith and got us on board the back of his van. We were off on a ride. He stopped and banged on every single door that looked like a hotel, inn or bed and breakfast that we passed en route to the centre of Bagan, asking for available rooms on our behalf, but there was absolutely no spare room to be found. At the end of the route was a hotel with a big lounge and a helpful receptionist with a big smile. He took us in and we retired to the sofas, and some fell asleep and had a nap. The receptionist came up with a plan: his sister had a hotel that was soon due to be opened. However, at present, it was still being constructed and had builders on site. He decided to get in touch and ask her if she could accommodate all of us. And then he had another excellent idea. He said we should hire a rickshaw and go to the top of the pagoda in the meantime. At the end of the day, the sunrise in the valley of the temples was the reason we'd all travelled to Bagan. It was about 5 am in the morning on the 30th December. We did as he said and went off to chase the first rays of sunlight before 2012 came to an end.

The steps were very cold and steep as we climbed the Shwesandaw Pagoda in our bare feet all the way to the top. Here we found a handful of other tourists and a few photographers setting up their kit. I stayed close to the other couple that I'd thought were Japanese, only to learn that the girl was from Japan but her husband was Vietnamese.

We sat around waiting patiently for the sun to rise. As it rose, the valley was uncovered in a golden glow, with thousands of temples seeming to rise up from below. It was a marvellous view, almost impossible to describe. It was a moment of love at first sight. And as we sat there watching the glittering light being reflected from the rooftops of those little temples, a thought crossed my mind. I'd previously read that this magnificent view was also known for hot-air ballooning, and it wasn't long after that in the distance, in the hazy light, giant hot-air balloons started appearing. It felt as though we'd entered an enchanting dream or a fairyland!

Once the sun was up our horse cart was waiting to take us back to the receptionist in the lobby where we'd left our stuff. He said that his sister could accommodate all of us, but with a condition: there might still be noise from builders at the site. Who cared about builders? As I was collecting my backpack and planning to join my new-found friends for breakfast, I saw the American boy on a bike and he was full of enthusiasm to head back to see the hot-air balloons and the pagodas again. It was a rare sight. I was hardly able to keep my eyelids open and this guy was full of energy speeding around on a bicycle like a maniac hungry for an adventure and like a little boy who's just discovered a new toy! He made me wonder and left me full of envy. It was the first time I'd seen someone else chasing the unknown and so full of life!

The following morning, his piercing American accent coming from the direction of the reception desk woke me up. I had to take a leap of faith, get dressed quickly and act. I was curious to know what his plans were for the day and to join him to discover what he was all about. I was happy when he said he didn't mind, and off we went to find another bike. His name was Himamauli, and there's a story behind that.

He was born in Kolkata to Indian parents and they moved to the United States when he was a little boy. They used to live further away from the city, in countryside nearer the Nepalese border, from where they could see the Himalayan mountain range. The peaks of the mountains were always covered in snow, hence the father granted his youngest offspring a meaningful name: 'The Son of the Snow-peaked Mountain'. It was the most bizarre and wonderful name I had ever come across in my life. Furthermore, I discovered that Himamauli worked at the White House in Washington DC. The timing couldn't have been better.

It was only a month before, in November 2012, that Barack Obama had been the first US president to visit Myanmar. Upon his arrival, he met Aung San Suu Kyi at a conference in Yangon. There was a fair amount of optimism and hope among the population for new reforms that would mark an end to the suffering of the nation after having been under a military dictatorship. I recall hearing the excitement of Aung San Suu Kyi being referred to as the 'princess' among the crowd and Barack Obama as the 'king' of the nation. The positive outcome of his visit lingered in the air among the native folks everywhere. Obama's visit opened the door to many foreign tourists eager to discover the mystical land that had been rarely seen by Westerners before, and it was a reason behind the hospitality industry being fairly unprepared.

After that morning, Himamauli and I became inseparable for the next three days. Side by side, we explored the valley of golden temples on bikes and approached the ancient monuments in complete silence, allowing them to speak to us. There was no need for the chatter of the outer world, just a pure state of feeling and being immersed in one's own soul. It was beautiful having someone by my side who understood the magic of silence in somewhere so mystical. There was an impression of being at one with it all, leaving the entire world behind.

In the afternoon we set off on the road of the less-trodden path and took a cab outside Bagan, climbing Mount Popa nearby. Throughout the journey we paused en route to drink tea and taste the most delicious sweets, called 'jaggery', and then stopped again in the village to watch a local's ceremony with children sitting on horses dressed in the most colourful gowns. On the way back, taking in the sun, exhausted and happy, we watched the world go by from the window of the car.

The following day we set out on the road to explore the well-known Inle Lake. We rose early that morning while the lake was still covered in a veil of mist and the shimmering rays of the sun swayed gently on the waves. It was a magical sight. The boatman steered his craft through long, thick grass that rose from the water creating a different kind of landscape. Everything was so surreal and pure. The floating villages made you feel like you were entering a land forgotten in time. There was a whole village of bamboo houses built on stilts. Throughout the boat trip, we stopped at silk workshops, a tobacco factory, gold and silversmiths, and we caught a glimpse of women from the Kayan tribe wearing long brass collars around their necks.

On our way back we paid a visit to a Buddhist monastery, and when the sun was dipping behind our sailing craft, a flock of seagulls suddenly appeared and took over the space above our heads as Himamauli fed them with some giant pancakes from the morning market... and I captured the image of this sight while the birds were flying about us.

At night, because everywhere was fully booked up in advance, we slept in the garages of a teak wood house with only a mattress on concrete ground and a mosquito net above our heads.

It was a hell of a fantastic adventure, the most spontaneous I have ever been in my entire life. I thought my birthday came a few days early that year, and it was the best gift I could have ever given to myself; the thought crossed my mind that hitting thirty wasn't that bad.

The day we spent on the lake was the 1st of January 2013 and the cover of my Lonely Planet guide had come to life in a way that marked a milestone in my life. The iconic picture of the Burmese fishermen was so symbolic of this corner of the world and it became another fulfilled experience.

When we reached the shore and got off the boat it was getting dark. I recall catching a glimpse of a couple in white linen clothing riding a bike – a thought crossed my mind and I said: "How the hell do they manage to stay so clean all day long?"

And Himamauli said: "That's exactly what I was just wondering about..." And then he added: "That is what I aspire to look like when I am old – wanting to travel around dressed in white." He'd taken the words straight from my mouth and we laughed.

Just for the record, nothing happened between us. The most intimate it got was having a line of knickers that I forgot about drying in the bathroom in a bed and breakfast. There was also that question of not knowing how old Himamauli was, not that age matters, but I was curious and afraid to ask. At the end of the day, I'd met a man who worked for Mr Obama in the White House and I felt honoured to have a friend like that.

And then he was off to the airport. We said our farewells and have stayed in touch over the years exchanging emails. Once he was out of sight it was easier for me ask. The emails make me laugh.

ME: You have never told me your birthday, btw. Not that it's important, but still good to know... I am guessing thirty-four going on thirty-five? Please clarify...

HIM: On my next birthday I turn forty-seven. Shhhhhhhh... don't tell anyone!

ME: Jeeezzz, your age. I didn't expect that, but HEY, what did your parents do to you, give you the elixir of youth? If you can maintain your enthusiasm and thirst for life then someone will have to kill you to get rid of your wrinkled old body! And please, I do not mean that in a bad way! I am only surprised!

PS: I am glad you are telling me the truth; if you'd said you were ten years younger I would have swallowed that without a doubt!

When I found out he was seventeen years my senior I couldn't believe it was true, but, hey-ho, age is only a number. What matters is the soul inside. The memory of that trip sank deeper into my mind, it being the best adventure and he the best companion I have ever had... and for that, I know the Universe had once again conspired for my soul to meet another of the same kind. Because if you allow yourself to be thrown into the unknown without any plan it will take care of you and create unexpected twists of fate way beyond your expectations.

On my last day in Myanmar, I woke up in Sunflower, the name of the hotel in Yangon I'd stayed at with the intention of making my last day in the country worthwhile. And before I left 'The Golden Land' I experienced the most mysterious day of all.

I checked my purse and noticed that there wasn't a lot of Burmese kyats left, but I wanted to spend the day without having to exchange any more, knowing I would be flying back to Bangkok next. Yangon is an industrial city and the most wonderful sight is the Shwedagon Pagoda, which I'd already visited. So I pulled out a map and looked at what should be the next point of interest. And I saw Kandawgyi Lake located inside a park that would make a perfect walk in the morning. So off I went to catch a local bus that cost peanuts, mingling with the locals.

On board the bus, standing in the aisle holding onto a bar among a crowd, a monk dressed in an orange robe sitting further up turned around and looked at me a few times. I looked back. What was he looking at? Surely he had seen a tourist in his motherland before? Then, when I got off near the lake, he got off at the same stop, came over to me and asked: "Do you speak English?"

And I said, "Yes." His eyes lit up, and with his broken English he explained the short walk away towards his monastery. We entered via a gate and he showed me a kitchen where their meals were prepared and brought two bananas for me to eat.

The next thing, he said: "I am calling my friend..." and adds something about a lesson or a class. Then he disappeared and came back with a mobile phone and held it pressed against my ear.

The voice on the other side said: "I am a teacher. Do you want to come and join my class?"

I said: "OK." The monk dressed in the orange gown gave me a look as if I was already a part of his master plan, unknown to me at the time.

He led me outside the gate and hired a cab and we headed

back downtown. We got out of the taxi, ran up a flight of stairs, and I found myself in a private English class and the monk disappeared.

There were about twenty nineteen-year-old Burmese students. The teacher, whom I'd spoken to on the phone, handed me a microphone and I stood in front of them. The reality of the situation started to sink in. Since I was an English-speaking foreign tourist, they wanted me to take over the class. I felt nervous but soon took on the role of a teacher and enjoyed the ride. I started by asking their names one by one and tried to repeat them, which was a hard task for me and we laughed. They asked me a lot of questions and I ended up telling them about my life; how I'd left for Germany at the age of nineteen, about my fashion studies in London and the decision I'd made on my thirtieth birthday to travel and discover foreign lands. They couldn't believe my age; I blame the colour of my skin for that. It was an interactive class and their knowledge of English was very high.

And then a girl sitting in the front row asked a question that took me by surprise. "Who is the most important person in your life?"

Everything went quiet as I was unable to decide. She'd caught me on the spot and I couldn't answer that... and in the silence of the class waiting for me to answer, she shouted out: "It's YOU! You are the most important person in your life!"

And I realised that she was right.

And then something else entered my thoughts, channelling wisdom I never thought I had as I started telling them that the most important thing is the love they carry in their hearts.

"If we give love unconditionally, it will come back to us tenfold and many times"

As the class came to an end, I asked each of them which was the country they wanted to visit one day if they had the chance... New Zealand, Australia, USA, Italy, France... and the list went on. There was a short pause, and I had a feeling that I'd said something wrong. I thought maybe it was easy for me to get up and go because I was born in Europe in a country where it wasn't hard to escape, but these Burmese kids might be subject to travel restrictions imposed by the government. But then, I'd lit a sparkle in their minds, and there's nothing wrong with dreaming and giving them the desire to follow their hearts.

After the class, I asked one of the boys to show me the nearest internet café, as I needed Wi-Fi to clarify my whereabouts. The young man told me that he came from a small village further afield and he'd arrived in Yangon because there were more opportunities there. He was staying with his relatives, and as a fresh graduate he was willing to take on any job that came along. I could relate to his journey and understood his aim to do well and I wished him all the best when we parted.

Once in the café, I realised that my hotel was only a few streets away. I went back, took a shower and decided to go to my favourite place to eat, one that I'd discovered during my first visit. The restaurant was forty-five minutes' walk away, along a dusty motorway in the heat. When I reached the place at 3 pm it was empty; I spotted only one man sitting a table away. When I approached the waitress and spoke out loud, the man turned around and said: "Oh, I can hear an English accent, are you from the UK?"

"Well, thank you for the compliment," I said. "I'm originally Slovakian, but I've lived in London for a few years now."

And he added: "Do you mind if I join you for lunch?"

"No, not at all," I replied, and I discovered he was American. I guessed he was in his late fifties, and he looked well groomed for his age. He joked that he hadn't had any cosmetic surgery on his face just yet. He was from Hawaii. I don't recall how, but we started talking about relationships – I always find it fascinating to hear what people do with their lives and love to listen to stories of all kinds. He said that somewhere in his mid-thirties he'd been hit by great depression as all his friends were getting hitched and had started having families with kids. He said there were certain expectations and pressures among the society where he lived and it was easier to fit in when married. As the years passed by, the only thing that was flourishing in his life was his business; he worked with jewellery and specialised in pearls. At the age of forty-five, he'd met a woman from Finland and finally married, and they had a son. After five years of marriage, she took their five-year-old son and left without saying goodbye. He couldn't understand why. He blamed her cold nature on the country of her origin and said that up in the north where they fish in freezing cold lakes people hide their feelings and are less able to communicate, which I thought was interesting. He said that he gave up asking 'Why' because he would beat himself up, and there was no point in doing that. He never found out the reason behind it all, but he did get to see his son, as they shared their parenting duties according to a plan they'd drawn up.

Now, later in life, he'd started to travel more and was enjoying the ride as he'd just come from Beijing in China and was here to attend the wedding of a friend in Myanmar. After he'd revealed his private life to me, he asked whether I was slightly disappointed hitting the age of thirty and travelling alone as a woman.

Well, I couldn't quite relate to his state of mind because I enjoyed being single and, in fact, I was having the best time of my life. I did mention that I had an open relationship in London involving J No. 3, who was sometimes there, sometimes not, but I'd known right from the start that he wasn't the one and so there were no expectations from either side... we were just filling the gap in each other's lives with a bit of romance.

We talked for a long time, and once lunch was over he asked if I would join him for dinner that night. I excused myself and skipped to the ladies, and the first thought that entered my mind when I came out was that we'd both enjoyed the time spent together so it would be best to leave it at that. It's not every day that you get a stranger's life story for lunch. And I smiled.

He was pretty understanding and said that perhaps he was trying to push it too hard. Instead, he decided to cover the bill for my meal, which worked out to be 6,000 kyats, exactly the same amount as his own lunch. And I thanked the man from Hawaii for being so generous and kind and walked away from the restaurant with the biggest smile. And in a moment of pure bliss and yet another example of synchronicity, I realised that I hadn't spent hardly any of my cash that day. I hired a cab to take me to the park where

Kandawgyi Lake was, which had been my target in the morning.

When I reached the park I bumped into another group of young students playing games there. I joined them and we ended up taking a photo with the class.

Just before the day came to an end, I walked into the final temple that I discovered. I recall a beautiful rounded ceiling in light blue covered with sea creatures – an octopus, starfish and exotic animals, with the elephant, unicorn and crocodile all swimming above my head in a sea of happiness.

At the end of the day, as I walked down the road following my map, it was getting very dark, as there were no street lights. The only flashes of light came from the cars passing by. I had no thoughts about my safety and still had some money left to hire a cab. At first, the driver didn't know exactly where my hotel was, but I knew that he would find my Sunflower because by now I trusted the Universe completely, as the whole day had been spellbinding.

Thinking about this day with the benefit of hindsight, I wonder if the Tarot reader in Covent Garden had been right? Maybe I really was supposed to be a teacher after all...

It was here in Myanmar that I'd experienced so much magic for the first time in my life. Every aspect of the journey seemed like a storyline, where one coincidence led to another and they entirely blew my mind. The word 'synchronicity' had never crossed my path until then. According to Wikipedia, synchronicity was a concept first introduced by psychologist Carl Jung, and it explains that events are 'meaningful coincidences' if they occur with no causal relationship yet seem to be meaningfully related. He introduced the concept as early as the 1920s but only gave a full statement on it in 1951 in an 'Eranos' lecture. Another term that stood out even more according to my own experiences was 'serendipity'. The definition of this word is 'an unplanned, fortuitous discovery'. As stated again in Wikipedia, the term was coined by Horace Walpole in 1754. He wrote in a letter to a friend that he'd formed the word 'serendipity' from the Persian fairy tale 'The Three Princes of Serendip', whose heroes "were always making discoveries, by accidents and sagacity, of things they were not in quest of."

# PART 2. THAILAND

On the day of my Myanmar departure I waited at Yangon airport for my outward flight to Bangkok. Here, I noticed another female solo traveller, walked up to her and made a new friend. L was from Switzerland, two years older than I was and a little more fortunate. She had been on the road for six months straight. After her adventures exploring countries in South East Asia, she was due to embark on a journey to discover New Zealand and Australia. We bonded from the start, revealing a little about our lives, and found out that we both had a younger sister that was married and a child in common. In contrast to that, we were both happily single with a string of past relationships and the odd broken heart. L did confide in me that she would never have walked up to a stranger to start a conversation just like that. I told her that the minute I saw her with the big backpack I knew she was a girl with a good heart. I never question my intuition when the feeling is right; my instincts were always very strong when it came to judging people's characters.

And I was right. For the next two days, L and I made a plan and explored Bangkok's main tourist attractions and sights, including a boat ride side by side along the famous backwater canals. It was fun to have a fellow companion again. And although I'm not a massive fan of big cities, and the heat and the noise coming from all directions, somehow I fell in love with Thailand's capital at first sight.

After two days in Bangkok, we ventured out and hopped on a train to explore Ayutthaya Historical Park, part of which is a recognised UNESCO World Heritage Site. Upon our arrival, we hired bicycles near the train station, which we had to take across the river on a ferry, and we had a wonderful day as we cruised around visiting temples and ruins of this ancient land.

After this adventure, L and I went our separate ways and I decided to travel down the coastline to Koh Chang Island. After three days of running around, all I wanted to do was to slow down and become a lazy beach bum. I didn't fall in love with the ambience of the island as such, but my little bed and breakfast tucked away from the noise of the main district had a large bed where I finally slept and had a good rest, and it was everything that was required. The other guests were mostly German families and pensioners. I didn't feel the need to interact; in fact, I enjoyed being silent and swimming in the pool enjoying the view, the lush palm trees, the sea and the most amazing sunsets. After five days of rejuvenation, it was time to move on and embark on a journey to Siem Reap in Cambodia and the highlight of the famous Angkor Wat.

# PART 3. CAMBODIA

The journey from Koh Chang via Trat to cross the border at Aranyaprathet, also known as Poipet on the Cambodian side, was a mission in itself that lasted a whole day. I might not describe the drama and the stories and scams on the border, but there is a tale about someone I met along the way that shouldn't remain untold.

This time it was Rosemary, who approached me on the ferry leaving the island. I learned that this lady was born in the UK but had lived in Australia and also in the USA. At present, she was travelling with no plans set in stone. Over the past summer, she had taught English in China, at a university in Wuxi. When the teaching summer course was over, Rosemary had decided to travel to India, where she'd spent three months. Sharing her adventures in this incredible land, Rosemary established a simple truth, based on her own experience, that India represents three F's – Filthy, Frustrating and Fascinating. She was sixty-five years old and said that she and her husband had worked all their lives to be able to travel once they hit retirement age. She'd retired last year. But her husband had passed away and never made it on the road. While in India, to avoid people asking about her husband's whereabouts, she decided to bring him back to life every time the question arose. She would say he was on a business trip and she had the time to explore during the day on her own. Despite this little invention of false facts, which were necessary to protect herself from inquiring Indian minds, Rosemary seemed to have enjoyed every step of the journey.

Listening to her story, I imagined the adventures of hers to be like those of the cast on the movie *The Best Exotic Marigold Hotel*, which I loved very much. Once she stopped sharing her tales, she turned to me and said: "What brought you on the road all by yourself?"

I told her about my journey so far and declared that I'd decided to travel across three countries in thirty days because of my thirtieth birthday – as simple as that.

Rosemary listened carefully to what I'd just said and then made a point: "So each day of your trip is a celebration of one year of your life so far?"

I thought that was an interesting way to look at it, because that idea had never crossed my mind.

Somewhere along the line since then, Rosemary sold the house she and her husband had once lived in along with all the possessions that no longer served a purpose in her life. It was only when she left the safety net of her past that she realised how liberating it was. I now learn about her whereabouts from group emails that she sends to all the acquaintances she met on the road, and this keeps us updated on her path. Fast forward five years, and I hear that she celebrated her seventieth birthday on the go and keeps travelling the world with no plans to settle down.

By the time we reached Siem Reap it was dark. I recall having trouble finding the cheap and cheerful little bed and breakfast that I'd booked in advance, but eventually I found it. The mission for the next day was to explore the ancient temples of Angkor Wat. You can book a tuk-tuk with a private guide to explore the site. I decided to rent a bicycle instead and discover the monuments by myself. And so the mission for the day ahead was to escape as many tourists as possible to allow myself to bathe in the essence of those ancient sites without the noise of the crowds. It wasn't an easy task! But I managed to find those small back roads with the less significant temples, and hidden roads where I felt I was the only explorer around, surrounded by nature and silence, basking in the sunlight, with a broken flip-flop, laughing at myself riding the bike for eight hours straight, finding the less-trodden paths and rejoicing every minute at the freedom of my existence!

For the rest of my stay in this little town, I decided to have some leisure time. One morning I decided to pay a visit to one of those mega commercial hotels alongside the main road and pay to use their gym and swimming pool. The problem with those humongous hotels is the fact that the tourists there never interact.

On another day I cruised around this charming little town with my beloved two-wheeled friend with nothing but the sun on my skin and the wind in my face and stumbled across the Peace Café. It was one of those tucked away hidden gems where you could retire with a book in a hammock for the rest of the day. There was a sign on the door about a yoga class that was taking place later on that day. I turned up for the class, but I hadn't realised I would get a full one-on-one session with the teacher as nobody else showed up. David was an American who'd fallen in love with Siem Reap so much when he first visited that he decided to relocate. Before his big move, he'd studied ballet, dance and taught yoga in New York City for over twenty years. He was extremely knowledgeable about how the human body moves, how it works and how it affects our wellbeing. I felt almost reborn when I left his class, and it was my first and best introduction to yoga that I have ever had.

As my thirty days in South East Asia were slowly coming to an end, I decided to undertake one last trip along the less-trodden path. I found out that within fifty kilometres of Siem Reap was a mountain within Phnom Kulen National Park. I hired a driver with a private cab to take me to the site, which was off the beaten track. He advised me ahead of the trip that it was a sacred mountain and a place of pilgrimage known among the locals and that the road nearer the site would be through a jungle full of rocks and bumps. I was already excited by the sound of that.

Once we reached the destination, we made our way towards the religious site, leaving our shoes behind. On the mountain was a large reclining Buddha carved into a sandstone boulder atop a giant piece of rock. My driver told me that this holy mountain was of great importance to Cambodians and was the birthplace of the Khmer civilisation. He further advised that the stone from which Angkor Wat is built came from where we were standing, and in ancient times the elephants carried giant rocks down the river on their backs to the site where the monuments reside today. I marvelled at the thought of that! It was a fascinating revelation that took me by surprise, and I felt truly blessed to have discovered it.

As I walked around, I noticed a beautiful young Russian woman with her husband by her side. I saw her the first time by the large Buddha; she was bowing down in prayer and she was crying. The next time I saw her was by a stall selling precious stones where she was haggling a price for a few small amulets. We exchanged a few words. She was buying them in secret while her husband wasn't with her. The third time I saw her was half an hour later walking past the path in the jungle and she was looking for the amulets she'd bought earlier, and now they were lost. Again she said: "Please don't tell my husband!" And she cried.

I marvelled at the amount of pain she must have been carrying in her heart and what the reason was behind all that. The one thing that sprang to my mind was that maybe she and her husband were unable to conceive a child, or perhaps he wasn't the right man and the Universe wasn't on their side. She was hiding the amulets she'd bought from her husband and then hiding again when she was trying to find them. If the love was pure, surely he would want to please her and give her those gifts from the bottom of his heart? After I saw her for the third time, looking for those gifts she'd bought and had lost and was running around like a lunatic in the forest, I thought, that's not freedom. Her destiny remained a mystery as I didn't see her after that. There's a saying that you should never judge a stranger because you don't know what goes on in other people's lives. I always wonder about the truth in someone else's heart.

Just before we left this sacred site, I saw a monk in an orange robe on top of a cliff and standing on a special carpet, and there was a sweet sound lingering in the air that added towards the mysterious atmosphere. I followed my driver's instructions and burned incense and gave offerings like the locals did. And I dropped to my knees in prayer, with the monk giving blessings. I had a wish... Deep down, I craved for a change from the London lifestyle that I lived... to something more nourishing...

Before we set off on the road, I was told that near this place within walking distance was a beautiful waterfall. My cab driver showed me the way and I decided to explore on my own. I passed a few locals going about their daily village life and soon I was walking along a narrow path tucked away in the lush green jungle and I started hearing the sounds of an enormous gushing waterfall. Beyond the lush greenery, the most beautiful scenery was hiding. There was a giant backdrop of cascading water tumbling down onto a bed of massive rocks hiding behind a veil of hazy mist formed from the water and the heat. I was fascinated by the sight of it. I found a huge basket adorned with flowers hanging from a tree and I climbed in. All at once I was transformed into a fairy tale, making me feel like Alice in Wonderland! As I watched local children bathing in the pool beneath the clearing, a simple thought crossed my mind: I love no man less but nature more.

***

The following day I travelled from Siem Reap back to Bangkok. Before I left 'The Land of a Thousand Smiles', with former King Rama IX grinning from every billboard in town, I explored a few more interesting sights. Among my favourites were the Vimanmek Mansion, built entirely of golden teak wood, and I fell in love with the silk prints in the Jim Thompson House. It was hard to say goodbye to the vibrant colours and the beautiful sun.

Upon my return to the UK, three thoughts entered my mind:

First: the smell of a freshly cleaned toilet at Heathrow Airport had never felt so good!

Second: sitting on the Tube in late January 2013 with freezing temperature outside and watching sad London faces felt like I'd fallen from a cloud and the whole trip had been a distant dream of a different kind!

Third: I should become rich – not for the sake of owning material belongings but to travel the world so I can watch the sunrise and sunsets in far-off lands!

# 14. Bali – Trouble in Paradise

It took me a while to settle down in London and come back fully to Planet Earth. I slept for twelve hours straight each night for a week. My body was in regeneration mode. And then a twist of fate brought about a change. I still recall the day in late January. It was in Starbucks on the King's Road where my former colleague S popped the question: "Andrea, I am going to propose something to you that could change your entire life. Do you want to come and join me in Bali to help to develop a fashion brand?"

I couldn't believe my ears. This is it, I thought! My mind travelled back and forth to the sacred site in Cambodia where I'd prayed for new beginnings with the monk. I was puzzled about whether the Universe had heard my call or was having a laugh again. Seriously, I thought the planet and the stars were on my side once again!

## PART 1. Bali Fashion Dream

A few days after this meeting, I was invited to visit S and her partner at their apartment in their South Kensington flat. The sun was shining bright, which is a rare sight on a winter's day in London. Their little puppy was excited to greet me at the door, wagging her tail happily. The flat was very clean and had a tranquil atmosphere; her partner was just finishing off his morning meditation routine. He was a true yogi, waking up every morning at 5 am for 'sadhana'; I believe this helped him to cope with his job in banking and to stay grounded for the day ahead in a high-pressure environment. In the living room in front of their couch, I noticed two beautiful huge rugs adorned with decorations that seemed to have meaning and a connection to Gaia – goddess of Mother Earth. Though I didn't ask about them, there was no time for that. He approached me with a question about the state of my mind. I felt tranquil and as blissful as I had been since I'd come back, and I was dressed in white. I sat down on the couch. S was on my left and her partner was sitting below a window on a chair facing me, the rays of the sun pouring in. He said: "Our paths have not crossed by coincidence. There is a window of opportunity opening up for us and we are destined to let our wings fly high and take the chance. After seeing your adventures in South East Asia in pictures on Facebook, we realised that you are one of us. We would like to offer you something that might change your life. It will be a new chapter for us and we want you to be part of that."

They had been together for seven years. S had been my manager at the swimwear boutique in the heart of Sloane Square for the past year. She was extremely focused and organised, and she never spoke about her private life. The initial idea for us was to help implement the manufacturing of the swimwear and loungewear for the company we both worked at. She had already spoken to the owners of the business and they were willing to go ahead and support the plan. The manufacturing in Bali would be cheaper than in Portugal, where the company was producing at the time. This opportunity would allow them to bring their margins down and increase profit on units of the merchandise. Her partner's role was to help us financially from the start, but his long-term mission was to concentrate on charity work and to help build orphanages and schools for unprivileged children in Bali and later also in India. The proposal for me was to join them and see where the project would take us from there.

Since Bali is an island with a very hot climate, they had it in mind to have a base in the north by the mountains yet close to the beach, so we would still get the sea breeze. The discussion went on about the fact that we as a human species can adapt to our environment very easily. The transition period and adjustment might just take a little time. But my mind wandered off in the

114

meantime into these beautiful surroundings full of lush green palm trees and the sea waves crashing into the shore at night.

A thought entered my mind.

"What about snakes? Are there snakes in Bali?" I asked. I was totally terrified of them – a recurring nightmare from my childhood.

"Why should you be scared of snakes? If you do not cross their path, they should not cross yours. In fact, they might be more scared of you than you think. Live and let live."

That was his advice. I'd only met this guy once before, when S came to introduce him at work the summer before, one Saturday afternoon towards the store's closing time. I remember his strong presence when he walked through the door. He was dressed in white linen from head to toe. S introduced each and every single one of us girls working on the shop floor that day; there was about five of us present. He shook our hands one by one, memorising each person's name while looking intensely into our eyes. There was something about this guy. He was the embodiment of grace and enlightenment. I wanted to be more like him. It felt like I'd just met Jesus Christ.

After the cards were laid on the table, I had time to think about their proposal and make up my mind. There was no rush in the decision-making, but still, it was on my mind day and night. I had to tell someone. It was a lot to take in all at once. Although I was advised by S not to spread the news too much as everything was in the planning stage. So I emailed Himamauli; he was out of sight and living in a different state across the pond – a safe resource for advice!

## Email from Himamauli, 4th Feb 2013

Yo, Andrea,

Crazy how things just fall your way!

Bali! WOW. Are you sure you're not a spy? It is quite hard for me to say whether it's the right thing for you, but it does seem interesting. Bali is totally wonderful – great food, people are very chilled, and it's amazingly beautiful and cool. It seems like there's a thriving business community and loads going on with exports to Europe and the US. But here are the questions a parent would ask: does it cost you money to be a partner? Or will you just be providing your hard work and 'know-how' about fashion and the industry? How reliable are the two of them? Can you just go there in August and check it out during a vacation – and then decide whether it makes sense for you? If so, seems like it's definitely worthwhile checking out … and if it seems legitimate, you can jump in knowing that it seems like a good idea. You should do what feels right. What are you thinking now after a week of thinking about it? Now I'm really curious…

## Email to Himamauli, 6th Feb 2013

Hola, Him,

I haven't spoken to them since last week. But yes, they are reliable, extremely reliable, I would say. I don't think they would tell me this without meaning it because it's such a big move and it's a plan for a year ahead. Her partner said that we would need to be completely honest with each other and act as one; everything would have to be discussed between us three; there would be no secrets. And yes, I can go there in August for two weeks' holiday to check it out first and then decide. I wouldn't need to invest money in the business. They said I would have a small percentage of the company and the longer I stay the more my share will grow. But they couldn't give me any numbers at this time because nothing is set up yet and they don't know themselves. But I still think that it's a chance that doesn't come around twice. To be honest, I have been fighting for my existence here in London for ten years now and still haven't achieved much or made savings because everything goes on my living expenses. And the idea of the dark grey London routine with one sunny holiday per year isn't that attractive any more. It is a bit scary because once I move out of London and leave my incredibly cheap room behind, there will be no turning back. The scariest thing though is that I would be cut off from my family completely. It's questionable whether I would be able to afford to see them in another couple of years, and it will be very hard on my mum.

My mind had already travelled all the way to the 'Island of the Gods', where the idea of tranquillity and a new life on an island was taking shape before me. I truly thought I was blessed to be given an amazing opportunity where I could combine a healthy lifestyle with work in my field of interest – the ultimate dream of combining the two greatest passions of my life. The thought of gaining experience working with the development of garments first hand on a tranquil island while having the balanced lifestyle, learning yoga and eating local organic food, sounded almost too good to be true! The Universe felt in alignment with the yearning of my soul! The answer was yes, of course. I couldn't let this opportunity slip through my fingers. I decided to give it a go.

S made a statement: "Andrea, this could be the line you draw into the sand to change your life." And I believed that.

***

Initially, the two of them were due to travel together to Bali during Easter time. But then the plan slightly changed. S was off first, and her partner was to follow her two months after that. At the same time, between January and Easter, the original business plan of running production for the swimwear brand we both worked at and eventually building up a sourcing agency was modified. I was a little surprised when I learned about this news from my former colleagues rather than from S herself. That was the first alarm that raised a flag. I felt annoyed that I wasn't informed about the change of direction and the purpose of my work responsibilities directly from S first hand, and I told her so. As I learned later, we were now to introduce a line of baby bags. She'd already made up a brand name for that. There was also the idea of developing a fashion line of understated glamour to accompany the image of the woman who would carry the lifestyle bag. Although S studied business with marketing and was terribly good at leadership, she made a confession to me that her dream had been to become a fashion designer ever since she was a little child. Well, I didn't mind that as long as we were to work in fashion, as I aspired to gain experience for my own growth in the creative field.

***

On Easter Sunday I went to the West End to watch a movie called *Cloud Atlas*, and it made me think soooo much. The message that came across is that a person's life isn't necessarily his or her own. It said that there will always be someone who will make us change our direction in life, our thoughts or even our paths. It said that a gesture of human kindness or a gesture of cruelty could create a ripple effect across the planet and this could affect humanity in one way or the other and the process could repeat itself time and time again. It also suggested that an individual should always fight for the truth, even if it might cost you your own life.

As I left the cinema, walking along the platform on Leicester Square Tube station, I spotted a woman of Asian origin with a short haircut. She looked identical to the character Sonmi from the film! She was a genetically engineered clone worker in a factory who one day stood up against the crowd and sparked a revolution. I was mesmerised seeing 'her' underground! My head was still in *Cloud Atlas...* It felt like she had stepped out of the movie and was in an extension of the storyline.

I would have to have a deep understanding and faith in myself that I was fulfilling my life's journey... or that I was creating a new one, a life I was to be a part of somewhere down the line. I thought there and then that maybe one day I would write a book about my journey, or maybe one day my life would change somebody else's life.

***

Suddenly I got news that Bali was off for now, at least the original version of Bali, as well as S's relationship with her partner, which caused quite a stir. They'd broken up. Right now my mind was full of doubt. S was still inviting me to join her, but the situation and set-up of things had taken a different turn. I would have to contribute towards the living expenses, which meant there would need to be a job on the side to support our venture in designing a fashion line. I felt like I should be looking into creating my own direction in life. W was trying to tell me that I could be anything or do anything I really want in life. AKS, my best friend, was creating her own company in Ghana and S had her own territory in Bali. At the end of the day, she was half Balinese and half American and heading back to reconnect with her roots. I didn't know whether I should go or whether I needed to find my own route.

And then I came to realise that I'd already experienced those feelings of uncertainty and anxiety in the past. I'd already given up the comforts of my former life for hard work and struggle in order to follow my calling to bring fashion into my life. People don't grow without taking risks in life. They say that everything happens for a reason, or that there's a reason behind all that's happening. And I decided to give it a go and see what the Universe had in store for me.

***

The latest updates on my move to Bali emerged. Due to the fact that S was there on her own with plenty of work to be done, she proposed for me to arrive in August as opposed to coming for a two-week vacation to start with and then decide. From the logistics and the financial side of things, it was an easier and cheaper option. I bought a one-way ticket to Bali and decided to give it a year and then see from there.

Suddenly, another change of direction in the master plan landed in my inbox. Alarm number two was raised. S had once again modified the direction of the brand. The baby bag and the lifestyle line for a modern woman was now history. It was revealed to me that we were to create a line of dresses influenced by *The Great Gatsby*, channelling the style of 1920's fashion. Furthermore, there was a new strategic plan with a crew on board that would make a documentary about the development of the fashion label as we went along. I started losing confidence in her constant flow of new ideas and the direction of the brand, but most of all the work I was expected to undertake. It seemed to have neither head nor tail. Being filmed while working is not my thing, and I asked for me not to be involved. I informed S about my discomfort and my concerns. Funnily enough, two weeks before my departure I had a vivid dream about a lion and a mouse.

**The interpretation of a lion and a mouse in a dream is as follows:**

1.  To see a lion symbolises great strength, courage, aggression and power. You will overcome some of your emotional difficulties. As a king of the jungle, the lion also represents dignity, royalty, leadership, pride and domination.
2.  To see a mouse in your dream indicates fear, meekness, insignificance and lack of assertiveness. You are experiencing feelings of inadequacy and fears that you are not measuring up.

I believe this premonition dream was alarm number three. I was the mouse at the mercy of a powerful lion, and I ignored the sign. At this time, I was arranging the international freight of my belongings to the address of a house in Denpasar where I'd put down half the rent for the year ahead.

Before I left the UK, I flew home to say goodbye. My mother, of course, tried to convince me to change my mind. Mum couldn't say no to me; she basically didn't have the power, even though she tried. She knew that once her stubborn daughter had set her mind to a thing or two there was no turning back.

The only thing I recall from this visit is something that kept

120

running through my mind. As I sat in the kitchen with her by my side going on about her daily business, I asked: "Mum, do you know what a man would do if he lost everything?" She ignored my question despite hearing it and carried on without noticing what I'd just said, so I answered for myself: "He would start again!"

## PART 2. House of Cards

On the 28th of August 2013, after almost ten years of living in London, I left my little room in Southfields and a secure job in retail behind me and I was off for new adventures on the Island of the Gods. I had my best friend AKS by my side at Heathrow Airport before departure. She was visiting London from Ghana. I felt truly blessed to have her in my life. She made up a mood board from photographs of all the crazy old times that we shared in the past. It was a very heart-warming gesture and I felt honoured and lucky to have a real friend like her by my side.

At the other end, once I reached the destination, I found myself at the arrivals hall with S screaming my name: "Andreeeeeeaaaaa, you made it to Baaaaliiiiii!"

We hired a taxi and it took us about twenty minutes to reach the house that S and I had rented for a year in advance. It had three bedrooms and an open-plan studio upstairs. It wasn't bad. There were still some builders finishing the bathroom on the lower ground floor when I arrived, but the location was in an industrial part of the city with no palm trees in sight. It was hot, sticky, heavily polluted and terribly noisy when you stepped outside. You had to watch your feet at the edge of the road; it was motorbike race madness from left to right.

There was a strange feeling taking over my thoughts that I couldn't identify at the time. I'd never felt like it before. Something wasn't quite right. I felt my heart was trapped in my chest. I felt as though I couldn't breathe, like my body was contaminated by a terrible disease. My mind was racing like the traffic outside and the air was so thick you could cut it with a knife. It was like I was experiencing death while still being alive!

My subconscious was screaming, what the hell have you get yourself into?

The following day I felt the same, if not worse. I'd had no sleep. I couldn't say a word. The internal battle with my subconscious carried on.

That afternoon, S stood up. She'd obviously had enough, and she said: "Right, we're heading to the beach." And I was glad. We both needed to get out of the suffocating house.

Once we reached the beach in Kuta, she went off for a run along the shore. I sat down on a chair under a palm tree and stared at the horizon. I was watching the sunset but my mind was full of darkness.

She returned after four hours and I was sitting in the exact same position as when she'd left. My brain felt like it was about to explode. She sat next to me, and I said: "S, I cannot do this! I'm sorry, it doesn't feel right! Physically, I can't." It was out!

"Andrea, the minute I saw you at the airport I knew that something wasn't right. Your negativity has spread and consumed the whole house. I had to get out," she said.

"I know!" I replied, and I didn't blame her for that. We both knew – the obvious truth was out.

The day after this incident two other girls arrived. One of them was her younger sister from the US and the other a beautiful young angel with a camera from Gloucestershire in England. She was on an unpaid internship for a couple of months to create visual media for the brand's launch. Although I knew I was no longer part of the crew, I was able to join the gang.

S called the house 'Rumah Impian', which in Indonesian means a 'Dream House'. Each day started with a morning ritual for building positive vibes, and the girls held brainstorming meetings for necessary action in order to hit the ground running.

One thing struck me. Had I not come to Bali I would never have realised that I needed a proper washing machine in my life! I had to come all the way to Bali to realise that clean laundry played such a huge role in my everyday life. How hilarious is that!

After a few days with the girls, I decided to go somewhere else.

I took a backpack, leaving my only suitcase behind, as I was still waiting for the rest of my belongings to arrive. My plan was to travel to Ubud in the heart of the island, surrounded by nature, and find solitude in an ashram.

In the morning, I jumped onto public transport full of locals and went to Kuta. There was a bus that could take me to my desired destination. At the bus stop I met a solo female traveller from the USA who had South American roots. We had a quick chat as we bonded right from the start and she gave me an address of a little homestay in Ubud where she'd just spent a few nights. I knew in an instant she was a blessing sent from the stars as I didn't have any reservations booked in advance.

It was evening when I reached the town and made my way to the place as advised. They only had one bedroom left, which was available for three nights. Perfect! I was sorted out.

During the night, at 4 am in the early morning, my phone started ringing like mad. It wasn't my family checking on my whereabouts, or AKS or J No. 3, who I was still in touch with… as a matter of fact, it was W. He'd called to find out if I was all right.

In the morning, the owner of the little place prepared sweet pancakes for breakfast with fresh fruit on the side. It was delicious, and perhaps I ate it all a little too fast. I was excited about the day ahead, as I was about to embark upon an adventure to reconnect with nature and take a walk among rice paddies for the first time since I'd arrived.

Trotting along on my own, approaching a village on the horizon, I spotted little bamboo huts with rooftops made of straw. I pulled out my phone and took a picture to remember them… and out of nowhere I heard a man's voice.

"Don't you want to be in that picture?"

I wondered where the voice was coming from. Suddenly, out of nowhere, a man appeared at the bottom of the path. He must been right behind me, unless he'd fallen from the sky. When he was close enough, I passed my phone to this mystery man and he took a picture, then he added: "Take off your sunglasses."

I nodded in silence and did as he asked. Then we started

walking side by side up the path among the small villages and we stumbled across a few local craftsmen displaying works of art outside their little bamboo shacks.

The man asked: "How long are you staying in Bali for?"

Hmmm, that's the question... that's the big question, I asked myself. "I don't know," I replied.

Further along we came across a small community with houses being built on a construction site. The mystery man stopped at each building while he shared a joke or two with the locals, and they all had a good laugh. I wish I'd known what it was all about.

"You know..." he said, "these men are from Java and they work bloody hard to make some dough to support their families that they've left behind." He continued: "You have to learn to speak the language of the local people and take an interest in understanding them and their culture, otherwise you're missing out."

At this point, I started warming to him as I began to understand the theory of his outlook on life and I felt happy to walk by his side. He said that most foreign expats move to Bali but they have no interest in connecting with the local way of life. Instead, they live in their own bubble and never make the effort to understand the Balinese language to connect with the locals.

I began to gain trust in this man and gathered the strength to tell him what had brought me here in the first place and the reason for me not knowing what was going to happen next... and then he started sharing a story from his life...

"When I was young I would travel to a foreign country and fall in love with the place and the surroundings of a particular land. I talked to the local men in the village and asked them how I could acquire part of their field – I didn't have the money to buy it back then. The village men said that if I worked hard enough and cultivated the field while growing my own fruit and vegetables for a year, I could earn my land with the work I provided. I was young, naive, hungry and passionate about looking after a field, hoping the hard work would pay off and the land would be mine as promised by the local men. And then, one fine day a year and a half or so later, I was working in the field as usual when this big black Range

Rover pulled up and this woman in a suit stepped out and shouted at me: 'What are you doing down there? This is my land!' I stood there not knowing what she was on about. Obviously, no one in the village had told me it was already pre-owned by someone else. Now, my piece of advice to you is that if you want to do anything in life, do it yourself! Don't rely on anyone else!"

Out of the blue, the man whose name I didn't know looked me up and down and said: "What's your problem? You're pretty and presentable, and seem to be looking after yourself well. You have all the elements to be successful in life. What are you afraid of? Where is your confidence?"

I thought about the things he'd just said, but the truth was that I didn't have the answers to his questions. I'd lost my self-confidence. Perhaps I'd lost it because I'd been rejected from the fashion industry so many times. Honestly, I felt confused and lost.

He interrupted the flow of my thoughts and added: "You have to believe in yourself. You can do anything you want in life! Stop being so fearful. Fear will get you nowhere."

We kept walking along the road and then he stopped and said: "We're about to enter private property that belongs to someone else."

"I don't mind," I said. Somehow I felt I could trust this man. I already felt perfectly safe in his company. We were standing in front of a heavy-looking carved wooden door, and when we entered, there was a stunning garden hiding inside. There was a marvellous little stream flowing alongside a lush green lawn next to a narrow path that led to a courtyard where, hidden behind palm leaves, there was a beautifully shaped pool and a small house with a glass door reflecting the atmosphere of this beautiful paradise. There were exquisite flowers and plants all around us. He picked one and passed it to me.

"Smell this one," he said. "The extract of the petals is used in Chanel No. 5." I marvelled at how he knew!

Then he said: "See? You're taking a risk with me, but the people who own this place don't come here very often, so don't worry. I know a local man who looks after this property. He won't be here at this time of the day."

My mind wandered off once again. Why would someone create such charming surroundings containing a serene paradise and a tranquil atmosphere if he hardly ever enjoyed the beauty of it all?

The mystery man interrupted my thoughts. "I'm looking for a butterfly that lives here."

And then he walked around a bush, staring at its leaves, but there wasn't a butterfly to be seen, so I asked him: "Is it a bad sign if you can't find that butterfly today?"

"Oh no," he said, and he laughed. "I'll see it another time." And then he started picking up all sorts of flowers from the trees and the bushes and the grass. He gave me two separate bunches, one in each hand. "Now you will place a bunch of flowers as an offering to a goddess down here and the second one you will keep until we reach a bridge across on the other side at the end of the gate. And I did as I was asked.

When we reached the bridge, he said: "Now, I want you to put all your fears, insecurities and worries within you into those flowers. Once you stand in the middle, throw it all away into the river!" Just before we reached he said: "Once there was a young woman who tried so hard to pass a medical exam to become a doctor that she was stopping herself achieving it... and she broke down in tears in the middle of the bridge..."

I did as I was asked while trying to hold onto the negative thoughts in my head before letting them all go as I watched the flowers disappear into the river.

As soon as I reached the other side I felt sick. A minute after that I was standing at the side of the road throwing up. It had all been a bit too much, or perhaps I was dehydrated from the heat or the pancakes at breakfast had been too heavy for me. Either way, the man was now standing patiently by the side of the road next to me passing over tissues and water for me to clean myself with. As lightheaded as I was, I felt a little sad. The mystery man whose name I would never know had wanted to invite me for lunch and introduce me to his wife. But sadly, after this unfortunate incident, my companion suggested I should take a taxi back to the place where I was staying and have a rest. He walked over to the road and stopped a car. I sat down in the passenger seat and started realising what a blessing it had been to have met him, and I thanked him for all his advice and kindness during our morning walk. In the meantime, he burst into a crazy laugh. It was hysterical and hilarious at the same time. It was real and surreal all at the same time. I wondered if he'd fallen from a cloud! I labelled him 'The Magic Man of Ubud', and I still can't get my head around about his insane roaring laughter!

I reached my little homestay, and after a brief nap I woke up and wanted to go back. So I rented a bicycle and headed towards a steep road on the hill where I'd seen him last, but he was nowhere to be found. I tried again the day after, in the morning, but with no luck. Instead, I went to visit a few other places, including the Neka Art Museum, which had a great selection of traditional Balinese paintings alongside more contemporary artists on display. It was a delightful experience, full of colour and light nestled in another peaceful garden full of beautiful plants.

Towards the end of the day, as I was speeding downhill on the bike, suddenly I spotted the 'magic man' riding a bike in the opposite direction on the other side of the road. I was sooooo excited that I shouted across the road and fell off the bike and broke yet another flip-flop. But it worked! He saw me and I ran up to him when the traffic stopped.

"How are you feeling?" he asked.

"I'm OK. Much better today," I said. "Thank you again for yesterday," I added.

"You see, you recognised a clairvoyant in me." And he carried on: "I was telling my wife about you yesterday, and she thought I should have taken you back to your hotel to make sure you were all right."

To which I replied: "Oh, don't worry, I was perfectly fine going back on my own."

The noise of the cars passing by was too loud and we could hardly hear each other's voices at the edge of the noisy road, but the one thing he did say was: "If you want to start anything in life, just make a plan and take baby steps, one at a time. There's no need to worry about what tomorrow will bring. Take each day as it comes without a worry in the world, and get rid of your fear. You can do anything you want, you're still young!" I thanked the man for his advice and we went our separate ways. I felt happy that the Universe had conspired for the two of us to meet once again.

***

The day after, I had already made plans to go to an ashram and stay there for a couple of days. In the meantime, I received a message from S that my belongings were at the Indonesian customs in Jakarta and I was expected to get in touch. I didn't quite like the sound of that. I'd been hoping to receive my stuff at the landlord's address where we'd rented the house.

I went straight to the nearest internet café on the main road. The news wasn't good at all. FedEx had my belongings at the Indonesian customs in Jakarta and had treated those five boxes full of my personal belongings, including three sewing machines, as 'white goods'. In order for me to receive them in Bali, I was expected to pay heavy import duty charges of 2,468.95 US dollars! This was an absolutely ridiculous amount considering I'd already paid the air freight company in the UK for the shipment and they reassured me that no further charges or import duties would be required upon delivery.

I don't even recall how I felt about it any more. The fashion dream had fallen apart like a house of cards and my life was being held in a storage dock! There was no way I was going to pay those custom charges to FedEx, that's for sure! By now I knew there was nothing for me to do in Bali, and sooner or later I would head back to England. Staring at the email on the PC screen, a wave of anger flushed over me!

My whole life was packed inside those five boxes. The machines weren't cheap; I had a five-thread coverstitch machine that was almost worth £1,000, another four-thread overlocker and a regular sewing machine too. But the most valuable things were my technical guides on how to make made-to-measure patterns for clothing that I'd gained during my four years' education in Slovakia; those were irreplaceable to me. Among other things, some of the best pieces of clothing I'd ever made were inside. But the most treasured one was a feather coat that I made myself from scratch during an internship with W – the fabric was a leftover from his A/W 2010 collection and it held beautiful memories that I treasured so much. Alongside my wardrobe, there were books, DVDs and diaries of self-growth and personal development that I'd written ever since I'd met the psychic. My life was somewhere in a harbour, currently on hold.

The owner of the internet café noticed that I'd become distressed and asked what was wrong. Well, I thought I couldn't lose much more, so I told him everything.

He was a good man who had lost his wife. It had happened when he'd worked as a print designer for a fashion brand in Japan. His wife was employed by the same company, working in the studio next door when she suffered a heart attack. He'd left his fashion career in Japan because the price paid was too high. That's when he came back to his roots and bought this little internet café in Ubud. I felt his sorrow and his acceptance of life as it was now.

A flash of lightning suddenly struck me. The situation I was in seemed ridiculous in contrast to this man's grief. He had been robbed of the love of his life – my problems couldn't compare to that! Thinking about it now, with hindsight, however crazy this might sound, I wonder... I wonder if the Universe planted this man into my day in order to ease my pain about the loss of my belongings. One can't feel someone else's pain but there are few words to describe such a thing, it has to be experienced. The tragic loss of this man's beloved wife was beyond my sorrow. He kindly offered to drive me to the ashram on the back of his motorbike without asking for anything in return.

\*\*\*

The ashram was set among rice paddies three kilometres away from the touristy crowd of Ubud. Upon my arrival, I received a warm welcome from the lady who ran this beautiful sanctuary. They held morning prayers followed by yoga, served delicious vegetarian food and offered gatherings with chanting and other rituals. I knew I was in for a treat, but I couldn't forget about my trapped belongings. Here at the ashram, I met a handful of other travellers seeking solitude in a peaceful paradise. There was a girl from the Czech Republic – a neighbour of my native land – an English student of psychology who had just returned from Australia, a Swedish man who was hiding from his fraudster business partner and an American storyteller who was simply enjoying her time there. I discovered that the Czech girl celebrated her birthday one year and a day ahead of mine. She was a smart-arse and worked freelance from her laptop. I envied her lifestyle. Soon after I left Bali, she met the love of her life, a companion and business partner in one, and embarked upon an entrepreneurial rollercoaster of a journey for twelve months across twelve countries. I grew increasingly fond of her intelligent mind, and we remained in touch.

I told everybody of my failed attempt to live on the island. Throughout my stay, I negotiated with the UK freight company with whom I'd initially shipped my possessions to get them sent back to London and drop the import duties raised by the third party as I no longer required them. The communication was slow due to the time difference and there seemed no solution in sight. FedEx demanded that the only way I could receive my belongings was to first pay the customs charges for their import to Bali and then request for them to be shipped back to the UK with export charges added, which sounded outrageous and useless all at the same time. On top of this ridiculous amount was a warehouse fee that increased day by day for storage facilities for abandoned goods.

My dispute was that I no longer needed my stuff on the island and I asked them to ship my belongings back to the UK and drop the unnecessary duty charges raised by FedEx.

It was a no-win negotiation for me. I was lost! It was full of nonsense and a rip-off! All they wanted was to make money, thinking I was some spoilt little brat of an expat with a thick bank account! The world is a damn money-making machine, I thought! And the Indonesian customs and FedEx were as bad! It was a helpless situation and I was sad. How could they do that?

Funnily enough, the lady who ran the ashram had a friend who worked for customs in the capital of Jakarta and offered her as a contact and tried to help. But this led nowhere and I was back to square one. I only learned that the Indonesian customs are among the most useless in the world!

I can't recall how long I stayed at the ashram in the end, but I remember cycling every day to Ubud and negotiating with the FedEx office to drop the charges. But this proved to be another pointless exercise.

Towards the end of my stay, I spent a few days with the girls in the 'Rumah Impian' house. We didn't talk very much about my struggle with my stuff and I was grateful for that. The last thing I needed was people feeling sorry for me; I'm not good at that. But before I left the island, the girls and I made it to the Sky Bar in Kuta, and I danced barefoot under the stars on top of a bar as I'd never danced before. It was wild!

On the 28th of September 2013, exactly one month after my arrival at Denpasar, I was on a return flight back to Bangkok. If we turn back the clock, it was only six months earlier that I was having the best time of my life during my thirtieth birthday trip, and now I was broke. It's no surprise that I call my Bali experiment a 'Trouble in Paradise' – the biggest crisis of my life so far.

## PART 3. The Downfall

Back in Bangkok I checked into the same hotel I'd previously stayed at, and it felt somehow comforting, like a real home in fact. It was good to be back. All I owned at the time was a suitcase full of T-shirts and shorts. There was one thing on my mind. I wanted to try to get a job in Thailand. Someone advised me to research craigslist online, which is like an American version of Gumtree in the UK. I looked it up and found out about an opening at Jim Thompson's brand. There was an advertised vacancy for a role in fashion development at the head office. My aim was to give it a last shot before I returned to Europe. I'd fallen in love with the legacy of his brand upon my first visit. He helped revitalise the print on silk industry in Thailand but his remarkable life story was what truly drew me in. Jim Thompson was an American who fell in love with the Thai kingdom in the late 1940s when he first visited. He invested heavily in traditional silk weaving, a craft that was slowly dying out at the time. He put the industry back on the map and became the ultimate 'King of Silk' and the most famous American living in Southeast Asia during this period. Originally an architect, he designed his own house, and it became an oasis of artefacts from six different regions of Thailand that inspired his work throughout his life. His house in Bangkok has since become one of the most visited museums among tourists. The tragedy of his sudden disappearance from Malaysian's Cameron Highlands on Sunday, 26th March 1967 remains a mystery. His body was never found.

I still recall the morning I was sitting on the back of a motorbike heading towards Jim Thompson's headquarters to inquire about the vacancy I learned about online. The air was hot and sticky, and by the time we reached the address, it was raining. When I arrived at reception I asked to see someone in the fashion development department to make an inquiry about the job.

The lady behind the desk looked me up and down and said: "Do you speak Thai?"

"No, I don't," I replied. The job description had been entirely in English and there was no mention of Thai nationality or language preference stated as a necessary condition.

"I am very sorry," she said.

No need to feel sorry, I thought. I'd pushed it too hard. Never mind. Once again I left with peace of mind because I'd tried.

\*\*\*

With no job on the horizon I soon left and was back in London. But before I started looking for a new job, I headed back to Slovakia to get some clothes that I'd left behind. It was cold. The first stop on my visit was my sister's house in the capital, Bratislava.

I was playing with my little nephew in the bedroom when she walked in and made a remark: "Andrea, can you tell me something?"

"Yes?"

"Can you please explain what the hell you're doing with your life?"

Tears filled my eyes. I already felt like I was falling to pieces, and her statement was the last straw. It was too cruel on my wounded soul.

It was the first time since the incident in Bali that I'd allowed myself to cry.

Now, I don't know if my tears started because of her statement or because of all that had happened to me recently. Maybe I was sad because I'd come to realise that nobody in this world understood the way I thought, including my own sister. She was unable to offer solace and empathy when I needed it the most. We were always very different. I had to swallow the fact that she would never be able to understand my choices in life, particularly the one where you had to fight for your existence in a foreign land. Her world of family security in the motherland was in direct contrast to the life I led.

I moved on to my parents' house in the countryside hoping for some peace and calm, but it was a far cry from that!

"I told you it was a bad idea from the start!" This was what my mother said for the whole time I was at home, like a broken gramophone record. She dug into me, trying to prove her point all day long. It was tough trying to escape her nagging voice.

The surprise came from my father, when he stood up and said: "Stop having a go at her! Can't you see she's already had enough?" It was the only comfort I had, and it came from my dad – I never expected that.

A mother should always try to protect her child, no matter how old they are, and I know she only tried to deal with the pain I had to overcome by making me responsible for my own actions. The words of wisdom from my childhood rang in my ears: "Go and do whatever you want, but if it doesn't work out, don't come crying on my shoulders." I always did things my way, and my childhood was ruled by wisdom gained through my own experience. My mum only reminded me of how she brought me up – the only way she knew. I honoured that way all my life and now I had to swallow my pride and suffer the consequences. I was like the bird in the story of *Jonathan Livingston Seagull* by Richard Bach, the one who'd flown higher than his own flock and came back only to realise he no longer belonged.

I was a broken soldier who'd lost it all, and I returned to a London that I'd tried to escape most of all! The city was my only home. Alone in the solitude of my own wounded soul, it felt like I had no family at all. I had to stop thinking that I should leave, because, clearly, for now, this was where the Universe wanted me to be.

***

I crashed onto my friend's couch; she would allow me to stay as long as it would take to find a new place to rent. W kindly offered me his flat to stay, but there was a new boyfriend in sight and I didn't want to interfere with that.

Luckily, the first secure thing that I got back was my job in the swimwear shop. This time it wasn't on the shop floor. I moved up a level and became the customer coordinator responsible for their website. At least I was going to learn something new in the field of retail via an e-commerce platform.

One week into my stay at my friend's flat I found a seven-bedroom house, this time in Norbury, not far from Streatham Common Park. My fairy godmother, one that I'd never mentioned before but who was always there when I needed help the most, made sure I was safe and sound. She and her husband lent me an electric radiator to keep me warm throughout the winter months.

They had a beautiful son that I'd looked after since he was in his mother's womb. The bond we created over the years is very strong. I call him my 'Wonderboy'.

The house where I stayed was huge, with a massive garden, an open-plan living room with a wooden floor and a kitchen in an Italian style. When I saw the room at the top of the house overlooking the back garden I knew I'd found my place at last. The only downside was the number of flatmates – there were seven of us, including myself. I saw this as a new challenge, of having to learn to compromise and adjust.

My first encounter with a girl who lived there took me by surprise with her first remark: "I don't know what you're looking for, but I can assure you, you won't find it here!" – Seriously, I couldn't ask for a warmer welcome, how bizarre!

I didn't say anything, of course. She was a Portuguese Goth. In fact, I took it all in and walked off in silence. Perhaps she knew something I didn't.

Even my best friend AKS told me off: "What the hell are you looking for, Andrea? Why can't you just be normal and live your life every day as it comes like everybody else?" Those were the words she said. It came as a surprise because I didn't know what I was looking for, or that I was looking for anything at all. I was truly unaware that people saw me as someone searching for something!

I later came to learn that the Portuguese Goth was put into an orphanage when she was born and adopted at the age of one by foster parents that she chose herself. There were six couples looking to adopt at the scene and she raised her arms towards her future parents upon meeting them. She was an interesting soul who introduced me to the author Dr Brian Weiss, who wrote the book *Many Lives, Many Masters*, which I treasured very much. And today I know she was brought in to cross my path with wisdom channelled through a message in the book that helped me to understand my past.

We should be patient and accept what comes to us, because the truth will be revealed when the time is right.

That was the lesson I had to learn. I was swimming against the current, trying to force a change to happen in my life. I asked too much and went against the natural flow. I tried to force a change in course and missed the red flags! And now I was back in the same old routine that I'd tried so hard to leave behind. The entire exercise had proved to be a wrong turn again. You cannot force a change to happen. You have to allow the change to occur when the winds of change are on the horizon. That's the time you should grasp it with both hands and take a chance. And not before or when you're against the clock. Because the Universe has its own divine timing and we should adapt to its course.

Regardless of the wisdom gained, I was still hurting inside and feeling a lot of pain. I had to buy a few things to settle in and I got myself grey sheets to reflect the mood I was in. The negotiation for dropping the charges of the import duty on my stuff in Indonesia was still going on. However, looking at the situation I was in, I made a final decision to cover all the necessary duties in order to receive my stuff back on the 1st of November 2013. Despite this decision, I had hoped they would drop some of the charges and I'd be able to get everything back.

**Notes from my diary, 9th Nov 2013**

It's getting colder. I'm questioning whether to start buying warm clothing or wait for my boxes to arrive. On the way back from food shopping dark thoughts are entering my mind. These thoughts keep coming to haunt me quite often lately. I'm thinking about suicide! I feel like it doesn't really matter if I'm here or not. Life every day is the same. And right now there is very little to look forward to. I cannot do creative things without my machines. I feel helpless.

One month more and it will be Christmas. I will be alone. They say that if you experience something bad you can either feel sorry for yourself or use the pain towards your own growth. I'm not feeling sorry for myself. I'm just feeling PAIN and I cannot feel otherwise right now. I'm not capable of feeling any other way. I feel hurt because my machines, the tools for expressing my creativity, were taken off me. Maybe the Universe is testing my will towards how badly I want to be involved in fashion. This is a test. They can take the tools, but they cannot take away your passion.

The thing is I don't know any more if I have the strength to fight. I wish I could have evaporated from this world without anyone noticing. I have seen some parts of the world... I have been in love... I have laughed and cried... I lived through happy and sad times. But the thing is that if I take my own life I would be stuck somewhere in between. But I don't want to be in between because I want to go to Heaven and from there look at my friends and family. I need to die naturally. I feel very sad. But I cannot push myself towards feeling any other way right now. The sadness has to run its course!

Towards the end of the month, on the 27th of November 2013, I received an email from the air freight company in the UK telling me that my belongings had been DESTROYED – deep sigh! Is this the end of the drama with Indonesian customs? Of course, my stuff wasn't destroyed but sold somewhere at a local market. As I had already been made aware, the Indonesian customs are among the most useless in the world. Maybe one day I'll meet someone wearing my favourite feather coat – there is only one in the entire world!

***

Today my thoughts go back to those dreams I had in the chapter 'Frozen Land'. The two dreams where my belongings were lost or left behind... even the palm-reading session in Covent Garden made more sense now. I became trapped in a foreign land... It makes you wonder... It makes me wonder. It seems it was part of my destiny and I had to pay a price to progress and to awaken my soul. The picture only becomes clear with the passing of time.

As for my family, I had grown beyond my parents' expectations of what my life should look like, to another level of aspirations, which were beyond my understanding at the time. I didn't yet have the knowledge of my purpose that I acquired later in life, which was to 'Simply Be'. Their perception of their daughter's life was for me to have a secure nine-to-five with a certain wealth acquired by the age of thirty with a house, husband and kids – the mediocre lifestyle of a common girl.

They couldn't grasp the fact that the suffering I'd experienced through the loss of my belongings and the failed experiment of living in Bali was, in fact, part of my attempt at personal growth. It was beyond their understanding and mine at the same time! And in that moment of no compassion towards one another's view of what one's life should or should not be, we had created a feeling of separation. It was a matter of time until I came to realise this truth. And I had to forgive them because my way of living was beyond their conventional thinking. The thought that rang in my head before I left for the island, the one I asked my mum, comes to mind: do you know what a wise man does when he loses everything? He starts again.

And so it was...

# 15. Learning To Walk Again

The year 2014 started off in a quiet mode. Truth be told, after the rollercoaster of events of the year before, I didn't want it to unfold in any other way. If anything, the aftermath made me more laid-back than ever before. The yin and yang in Chinese philosophy came to the surface as a natural law. Somewhere in the depths of my heart, the pain passed, and I was hungry to make my life worthwhile again. I made a simple resolution to fill my heart with happiness.

But before I could fully commit to a new quest for being happy at all times, I had to heal my past. I recalled the episode when I'd met the psychic in the first chapter 'Beacon of Light'. He'd declared that the only way for me to understand life was to research the spiritual realms of existence, and only in this way would I reach balance day in and day out. I had to travel that path to understand the mysteries of life so I could heal my wounded soul to allow freedom to enter my mind and let the Inner Child smile again. At the end of the day, happiness is the key to life.

***

London is a large melting pot of people from all walks of life. However, you can easily become isolated if you don't mix with the crowd. Social media has made it easier for the masses in the city to connect with one another. I have joined the 'Meetup' app, which was designed to connect people who share the same hobbies and interests. Through this network I found a small group called Spiritual Alchemy, who were focused on healing and transformation. We were still in the winter months. It was cold outside. But the minute I stepped through the door in the basement of a community centre not far from King's Cross St Pancras, a wave of warmth and calmness washed over me. The light was dim and there was the fragrance of scented sticks lingering in the air. People were sitting in a circle, so I sat down quietly and joined in. As with any group of individuals who don't know each other, we had to introduce ourselves and say a little something about why we'd decided to come along that evening.

The following story was anything but a balancing act to soothe my Inner Child. But at least I realised I wasn't alone. We are all on board on the same boat wherever we are in life. And life and death are never too far apart. The first girl that caught my attention introduced herself.

"In three years' time, I will hit forty. I'm single and I haven't managed to build up a career. In fact, I feel completely fucked up, because I have no idea what I am supposed to do with my life."

The last girl in the circle, originally from Poland, said: "I have lost my mum to an illness, and my brother couldn't bear it so he took his own life. My dad passed away last year and I keep asking myself why they didn't take me? Why am I still here? I wish I was there… I wish they'd took me with them!"

There was utter silence in the room when she finished saying that. It was beyond our wildest imagination how much pain she'd had to endure. None of us had experienced such hell before. Her life story wasn't something you came across every day. It was impossible to watch and not to feel her loss. Pain was etched across her face. I was mesmerised. The girl had no desire to live, no spark in her eyes… she was in a deep, dark void. She was physically present but her soul was struggling. She was torn and she was lost. And we couldn't imagine the amount of suffering she was going through.

All we can do in a situation like this is to offer solace, but the greatest challenge after such a tragic loss is to turn inwards and allow the pain to run its course, and hopefully one day we wake up and find the strength to say that enough is enough, and to change our mindset, and to shout out loud, I am here, I survived! This, however, requires time, if not a lifetime. I am a strong believer that the Universe wouldn't give us such a challenge if we were unable to survive. Life is a test, and the victory belongs to those who survive.

Coincidentally, those two girls and I were put together to work in a group of three… and that's when things got a little out of hand.

We were asked to tune into one another's energy and provide channelled guidance to support each other. The girl who spoke first and I had to console the girl from Poland to help to soothe her grief. I'd never done such an exercise before. We sat there in silence. All I could sense was a very cold atmosphere that gave me shivers down my spine, and I saw shades of grey and darkness everywhere. Then the other girl blurted out: "I see a square grey house… I'm going upstairs, and there, under a window, is a chest of drawers. On top of this chest of drawers is a doll. You need to go to the house as there's something left behind for you in that room. You have to go and get it. You've left something behind in that house…"

After this revelation, the girl confirmed that the house in Poland where she grew up with her parents was grey and square; a lot of Eastern European houses are built this way. She used to have her own room and a doll when she was small. But she didn't know about anything that she'd left behind. The other girl insisted there was something that she had to go back to find out. At this point the two girls joined their hands, embraced each other, and the one who had channelled those images burst into tears on behalf of the wounded soul. These were tears of genuine sadness for the one who had lost her family and was unable to shed a tear to relieve the pain on her own. She wasn't ready yet to let it go… the hurt was too deep to swallow.

The group looked to see what was going on; we all felt compassion and genuine sorrow. And at that moment a sense of oneness took over the space – we couldn't replace her family members, but the warmth and the safe environment hopefully provided some balm for her soul.

And in this moment of revelation, we discovered that the girl who thought her life was on the rocks had a natural gift to see *beyond.* It was interesting to watch.

When the two girls turned towards me, she said she saw mountains peaks that were unique – some kind of yellow stone with ridges all over it – and there was a wooden bridge. It was in some far-off country, but she was unable to identify it. Funnily enough, she said that once I crossed over the bridge I would meet a man – if not a husband – and I laughed.

The next day I received a message from this girl. She forwarded a picture of the mountain that she'd channelled for me. "It's Mount Huangshan – the Yellow Mountains in China that I saw last night…"

I don't know why, but China was always on my bucket list. I found the unspoilt nature of the countryside full of mystery, and this girl with a gift to see reminded me that I should undertake this journey and make it a once in a lifetime trip. These breathtaking images of Huangshan Mountain in China were calling me.

I haven't stayed in touch with the wounded girl from Poland, nor do I know if she ever went back to her house to find out what was left behind, but I learned from word of mouth that at the age of thirty, a few years down the line, she went off to celebrate her thirtieth birthday in Dubai, and I was immensely happy to hear such news and strongly believe that she was on the right path towards recovery!

After losing my stuff, I made a promise to myself not to hoard too much crap. Material stuff had somehow lost its meaning in my life. I decided I would travel more and invest all I earned into experiences to enrich my life. Yet I was unaware that the messages from the other side, from the spiritual realms, would guide me on the road once again and enrich my life in the most peculiar way.

# 16. Mount Shasta Retreat

Soon after those incidents with the Spiritual Alchemy gathering, I joined forces with the girl that had a gift to see and together we discovered the London College of Spirituality (LCS). This was another social network of like-minded souls. They used to organise an event called 'Healing Night', which was held once a month on a Friday night. They were run by two leaders who'd founded LCS and a handful of volunteers that specialised in reiki healing. During those sessions, the warm touch and gentle flow of energy from them felt very soothing. After the sessions I felt more grounded and at peace with everything – a deep sense of relaxation overtook me. I remember the time when I arrived for the very first time and one of the leaders approached me and revealed that deep inside we are all healers, we just need to find that healer within ourselves and learn to nourish and transcend the gift. Soon, the crowd that joined those gatherings started to feel like a new-found family.

It was here that I learned about the sacred site of Mount Shasta in Northern California. I knew by now that it wasn't a coincidence; I was on a quest towards healing my wounded self, and the Universe was showing me the way once again. The London College of Spirituality was organising a retreat to the site and I felt it was necessary for me to undertake it in order to let go of the past and move on to a new chapter in my life. China had to wait for the time being. I had to take the chance that was presented and allow the natural flow of events to unfold. I heard this call and didn't want to let it go. This was the trip I'd been waiting for. I was really curious to find out how the sacred area of Mount Shasta would enrich my life. The people who had been there before kept saying that once you hear the mountain calling your name, your whole life will take on a different turn.

The legend has it that Mount Shasta is one of the most sacred places on Earth. It's considered to be the location of a major intersection of ley lines and a powerful spiritual vortex. Our ancient ancestors knew about those sacred locations, and they gathered together and held ceremonies and rituals to harness their powers. It allowed them to access higher dimensions of consciousness and intelligence. It's known that there are seven main energy centres in our bodies and the same number of vortex points at locations around the world. Mount Shasta represents the root chakra within the energy of the body. It is our foundation and the keyword is survival. The rest of the chakras – sacral, solar plexus, heart, throat, third eye and crown – are equally powerful.

Before I fully committed to this trip, there was a challenge that I had to deal with. I fear crowds and I'm no good with larger groups, so this would be a learning curve. We were an organised group of thirty-seven from London seeking light. For someone who loves to travel on their own and go with the flow, this was a hard cookie to overcome. But those 'lightworkers' proved to be a different bunch; they felt more like my tribe. And in preparation for this trip, worried at not being part of the crowd and feeling the need to be accepted by them all, I made thirty-seven orange scarves with four colourful stripes representing the elements of Mother Earth in brown, indigo, red and light blue.

When I told my mother about my decision to go on this trip, she shook her head in disbelief again, thinking I was turning into a lunatic. She was utterly convinced that her daughter was going to be brainwashed by some cult in an American forest. I couldn't comment. I knew I was on the right path when my bill for the last food shopping before my trip added up to the value of £11.11 on the receipt. Once again I turned to numerology to unleash the hidden message behind all of this.

The number 1111 is often referred to as a wake-up call or a code for activation. The Universe has acknowledged you and wants you to be aware that help is on the way. The Universe only reaches out when you need help, so you'll likely instinctively know what the problem is that you need help with. When you see the number 1111, the Universe is sending a signal that an energy gateway has opened up for you.

***

We embarked on the trip in September 2014. Once we landed at the Redding Municipal Airport in the middle of the night, we felt a different kind of energy; the vibe was something else. It felt like being on a different planet. The town near Lake Siskiyou where the retreat took place had the friendliest crowd I had ever met. It was very common for a stranger to pull up in a car, lower their window and say 'good morning' with the biggest smile.

The Shasta retreat turned out to be a hell of a ride, an experience that felt like a lifetime. The week was packed with raw emotion, as each and every one of us was opening up their own personal scars. We were thirty-seven snakes shaking off an old skin. Each morning, workshops were held to allow people to open up and face their fears... to see beyond the visible... to uncover the mask, layer by layer, to unleash all that was left beneath and let ourselves be seen for who we truly were. We saw tears of sadness and joy, happiness and sorrow, darkness and light reflected like a mirror in another's soul. As we progressed and allowed more light to penetrate within us, the journey started to reveal beautiful encounters and synchronicities.

At the start of the trip, we paid a visit to mineral springs to wash the impurities from our bodies. It was set in peaceful surroundings in the middle of a forest and the waiting room had wonderful books to read. I found a message hidden within one:

Red Coral please remind me of the blood of all my kin.
Each of us has feelings that reflect the joy within.
May I nurture my own needs, then learn to share in turn
The love that is my essence.
The heart that in me burns.

145

There was also a powerful session with a local healer. She activated our bodies with a quantum vortex technique aimed at soul-body integration and accelerated personal evolution. One evening we were invited to an intimate concert featuring a beautiful fairy dressed in a long white gown. She played a piano and sang enchanting songs with the voice of an angel. We sang our hearts out, and that evening belonged to us. There was a line that became a symbolic embodiment of that memory, and we chanted this mantra for the rest of the trip: "All I ask of you is to remember me as loving you."

The programme allowed us to take part in various activities nearby and have a rest at the same time, embracing the pure natural surroundings with the mountain in the background overlooking us like a beacon of light. Lenticular clouds hovered above its sacred peaks. The morning started with the sun shimmering across the lake, sparkling like a diamond. We took walks in the forest of giant pine trees and took a swim in the lake. One day, the clouds formed the shape of an eagle. That afternoon I walked in the forest with my friend and asked her to take a picture of me at the lake with the eagle above my head. I stood there, raising my hands up to the sky with my palms in the shape of a heart. She zoomed in with the camera and said: "It won't work. You're shadowed by the trees so you appear in the dark."

I shouted back at her that I didn't mind. And in the next split second the sun came out from behind the trees and my body was completely lit up.

"There is a light!" she shouted. I have a picture of me in the dark and one in the sunshine, like yin and yang.

At night, we had a campfire and the stars were shining so bright and looked so near it felt almost possible to reach out and touch them.

Throughout our morning gatherings, in the common room were scattered decks of oracle cards with messages inside. The two that revealed themselves to me were an 'Action' card and a 'Sacred Pool'. I knew I wanted my life to take a different turn, yet I didn't know how. Strangely enough, throughout my stay, I woke up in the middle of the night and the display on my phone would show '00:00' and my mobile would be frozen. I thought I needed to start my life from scratch. This happened at least two or three times. The Action card had a picture of two horses running through a field and the meaning is revealed here:

This card tells you that now is the time for more aggressive forward movement. The galloping horses represent intentional and concerted action directed towards your goals. It shows you are on the right track, but your determined efforts must be increased. The white horse is an inner action of spirit and thought, the black horse is the outer work that still needs to be done. So continue taking action and trust your intuition. In time, you will break through and see the results you have been working so hard to create. Create a structured plan, and then make sure you take daily action. This will move you closer to your goals. Be flexible yet persistent – and ever conscious of your ability to act on your own behalf.

The Sacred Pool card had a powerful meaning too:

The world is a reflection of your thoughts, feelings, and beliefs. Embody the love you wish to see in the world. When you look into the mirror, do you like what you see? The Sacred Pool asks that you focus on self-love and self-esteem. We are all works in progress, so a detached self-examination made with rigorous honesty is called for now. Reflect by the Sacred Pool and be at peace with yourself. Can you see how far you've come and how magical your life is? Do you notice the spark of the divine shining through your eyes? When you are conscious that you are an embodiment of Spirit, it becomes easier to respect yourself and act in good conscience… then you will reap the greatest rewards. Your unique service to the world is not only needed but celebrated. See the love within you, and know that if you cast upon the waters, it will return to you tenfold. Be at peace, for you are beautiful and loved. Act with surety and confidence, and success shall be yours – whatever your inquiry.

Towards the end of the trip there was a funny encounter during our visit to a crystal shop where we had a session of healing sounds with crystal bowls. The sounds of the singing bowls had powerful energies, although I recall having fallen asleep. Nevertheless, this little gem of a place was bursting with precious stones from all over the world. I just felt a little overwhelmed and unable to decide which one to take. In the end, I decided to ask the man at the till for his advice to help me to choose.

This is what he said: "You have to ground yourself."

Hmmm. I wasn't sure how, so I asked: "But how do I do that?"

"Just stand here, close your eyes and say to yourself, 'I am here'."

I tried that. I even had to say it out loud a few times in front of this man in the middle of the shop with my eyes closed, but somehow it didn't work.

And the man said: "You are not physically present here..."

And I freaked out... and asked: "Is that bad?"

And he laughed and said: "No, it's not bad if that's who you are..." So he advised me to go and sit down on a bench made of a special rock that would help me to ground myself and then after a while see which stone I gravitated towards.

And so I did as I was asked. When I got up I caught a glimpse of a little blue heart. It was lapis lazuli that I felt drawn to, and I walked up to the man and asked what he thought about that.

He said: "If I had to choose, this is the stone I would pick for you. It's a stone that's been used since the beginning of time. It symbolises intuition and resonates with truth, enlightenment, and it stimulates the third eye."

I walked out of the shop feeling even more enlightened, despite being accused of having been withdrawn physically.

At the end of our trip, we held a ceremony at the foot of Mount

Shasta. It was a beautiful evening full of joy and laughter, with drumming and dancing around a fire that we built until the sun went down beyond the valleys. Everyone felt liberated and free. People's faces radiated with heartfelt energy.

On the last day before we left, we held our last gathering standing in a circle gazing into each other's eyes while we sang: "All I ask of you is to remember me as loving you." The thirty-seven of us created a bond as strong as one of true blood. I received beautiful messages from my fellow 'lightworkers', with encouragement to continue with my spiritual quest. At the end we were asked to describe in a few words how we felt after all that we'd experienced in the week that had just passed. I was short of words to describe on the spot, but then I remembered! I remembered what my mother has said just before I left. She feared her daughter would lose her mind in an American forest... And then it hit me hard... she was partially right! I was beautifully brainwashed, like an innocent child. I had gone there to unlearn everything that I had ever learned and to leave all my fears behind. It felt like being reborn again from the base of my root chakra.

*** 

Once we separated I decided to go to San Francisco to explore for a day. But the minute I touched back down in this city I was in for a tremendous shock. The contrast in the surroundings I found myself in added to my confusion. There were no more giant trees, only a long concrete strip and enormous man-made machines. The hotel room I stayed in was facing the runway, with aeroplanes flying in and out before me. I was staring at this through a wall of glass that felt like a giant screen. I was an alien misplaced in space. The energy had a turbulent feel. The child who was learning to walk in this big wide world felt confused once again about where it belonged. Somehow, I fell asleep.

The next day was an early start as I ran around like a headless chicken while ticking off all the places on TripAdvisor's must-see list. The sun was behind the clouds but I managed to get a decent picture of the famous Golden Gate Bridge. And towards the end of the day, I found a sculpture in the shape of heart in the middle of a square and felt connected once again… as if the mountains had sent off their last farewell.

For the rest of the trip, I became an urban citizen of New York streets. I paid for a visit to see J No. 3, who had relocated to the city. As a matter of a fact, W was moving to the Big Apple exactly that same week. We met as soon as he arrived and hung around Manhattan the whole time. He introduced me to one of his friends who worked as creative director for a famous New York fashion house and we stayed at his place in Soho for a couple of days. It all worked out like a fairy tale. We browsed the streets, visited members' clubs, markets and galleries. I felt fortunate beyond words, like a princess being looked after by them all.

On the last day before I left, W confessed that my presence had made it easier for him to settle down into his new environment… It was all meant to be.

Himamauli, who lives in Washington DC, couldn't make it to see me, but he left a message instead: "Andrea, enjoy the skyscrapers. It's a different kind of Zen…"

And I think I did…

# 17. Quest for Change

Upon my return to the UK, the first positive change that took place was on the home front. It was inevitable. I still resided in Norbury with those seven flatmates, and the atmosphere was often quite shaky. When I returned from NYC, my childhood friend from village next door that lived in London announced she had a spare room for rent in Streatham Hill after her flatmate had moved out. The timing was just right. I moved in with a girl I'd known all my life, the one I'd sat next to in primary school and hadn't talked to as we were both equally shy. After living here for nine long years with people from all over the place, it felt like I had a real home at last. The flat was number five.

*** 

The year 2015 started off on a happy note. In May I invited my mother on holiday to Greece to strengthen our relationship. I had to teach her how to overcome her fears and push boundaries, as she'd never taken a flight in her entire life and was scared of it. The plan was to show my mother where I lived on our way back, but once again the Universe took me on a different turn...

During this time, W flew from the USA to spend a few days in Barcelona, and he invited me to come along for a long weekend. And you don't say no to that! The morning after my mother and I arrived from the island of Kos, we took a cab back from where we landed the night before. My mother was sitting on a return flight back to Bratislava while I was jetting off to the city of Sagrada Familia. She didn't mind, her head was still spinning from the beach holiday on the Greek island! She later bragged about this trip as the best one she'd ever had.

In the meantime, I was invited to stay at a swanky hotel in one of the coolest European cities around! W and I stayed in a giant suite on the top floor of W's hotel. The view was to die for. I felt privileged!

Upon my return from Barcelona, there was a surprise when I got to the door. I was locked out of my flat and didn't realise I was missing a key that my flatmate had. She was also in Barcelona but on a later flight, coming back at midnight. Unable to get in, I banged on every door in the house but no one was around... No one apart from J No. 5 in the basement flat. He'd just ordered a pizza and asked me to hang around on his couch until my flatmate arrived. I'd never met this man before in my entire life. The rest is history...

Two weeks after this incident he invited me to a stand-up comedy show. The act was an Irish comedian who'd lived in China for three years and based his performance on this experience. It felt similar to the trip I was planning for the year ahead. So I said yes to the date and off we went. It was developing like a plot from a romantic comedy. Everyone at work thought that J No. 5 from the basement flat was finally Mr Right, but in the end it didn't work out. The Action card from the Shasta trip occupied my mind. I had to give it my best shot and try my luck before I gave it all up!

I still recall standing in the side alley behind Sloane Square while an overwhelming feeling of helplessness took me over. I had three job offers, but none of them led to my desired goal of becoming creative, but rather were supporting roles in various fields. The first role was for a retail supervisor at a high-end luxury womenswear boutique, the second for an upcoming yoga studio as an e-commerce leader, and the third role was as a junior production assistant for a luxury fashion brand. I had been working my entire life trying to break into fashion design while pushing the boundaries and this is what I got? Those three opportunities felt like a crossroads and none of them led to anywhere near what I wanted to do. I had to take what was available at any given time to be able to survive. It hadn't hit me until then that at the age of thirty-two I was getting nowhere! I stood there flabbergasted, questioning my life. It was a hot sunny day but I couldn't see clearly through my tears. So far in my life I had been fighting for something that seemed unattainable.

It had taken me six years since my graduation in 2009 at LCF to get a junior position in something that interested me. I started my new job as a production assistant at the luxury fashion brand for the East London womenswear label in the summertime. This was the closest opportunity to what I was aiming for but was still a long way away from my goal. It wasn't as creative as I would have liked. The transition starting from the bottom wasn't an easy task. I had to move down the ladder from my previous post. I remember a significant dream prior to my new role that captured the way I felt.

*I was a sheep – an outcast sheep. In order for me to join the rest of the flock, I had to climb a fence so I could join them. So I did, and I clearly remember the feeling after climbing over the fence – I wasn't a happy sheep. I felt rather small and insignificant among the bigger sheep. Once again, I felt as if I didn't fit in.*

My desire to work in the fashion industry was losing its grip on me.

Once you start questioning something you believed would make you happy because you'd waited for it almost your whole life, well that certainly throws all your values off balance! This was the state of my mind at the beginning of the job.

**Notes from my diary, 2nd August 2015:**

What if fashion is not my true path? What if there is something else for me to fulfil in this life? For all these years I have been waiting for my career to take off, and I have sacrificed a lot. There was a time once before when at the end of my strength a little star – a beacon of light – opened up a new path towards discovery. My second awakening took me on the road to discover Nepal, where I asked whose was the voice that pushed me on the road to explore more of my soul in places unknown to me, and off I went to Myanmar, Thailand and Cambodia to travel some more. And through this journey I have discovered my passion for the unfamiliar, for unpredictable adventure, and most of all a deeper path of self-discovery. And then I lost my possessions in Bali and had to go to Mount Shasta to heal emotionally, and here I am now questioning once again what is the purpose of my life? It's all a mystery. If fashion isn't the way forward and it doesn't bring satisfaction to my life, I may as well give it all up and start looking for new path in my life. I just want to be happy at all times.

One day at work I looked to the sky through the office window where I sit and then back again across my computer screen when a message suddenly appeared staring back at me from an unknown source: 'When was the last time you created a piece of work that truly mattered?' There was something... something I ought to do, and I didn't know what that was! The message was a trigger. The answer was unknown at the time... I wanted to know... Badly!

After a while, I slowly settled in and realised what a wonderful bunch of people I was working with. If it hadn't been for the team, I wouldn't have stayed. As the festive season slowly began, I skipped the switching on of the Christmas lights. This was a dressing-up occasion at the flagship store in the West End.

The next day they asked: "Andrea, why didn't you come and join us last night? – You should have! You're now part of our family!" The dream with the sheep came to the forefront of my mind. With that statement she made me feel welcome and appreciated; my little sheep now belonged among the bigger family. And a feeling of warmth came forth at the realisation of it all, and I smiled...

# 18. Garden of Happiness

Towards the end of the year, I needed a break from it all. My thirst for adventure was hard to ignore. I booked a flight to 'The Land of a Thousand Smiles' and spent Christmas in Thailand. This time I explored the Krabi islands. I wasn't alone. When I arrived, my flatmate friend from childhood was already there. She was afraid to start with, but she stepped forth knowing that I would come along. It was her first solo trip.

When I stepped off the long-tail boat on the west of Railay Beach, I waited for her to arrive from the east side of the strip. When she finally appeared... Wooow! Seriously! What a surprise! A goddess was walking down the narrow path towards me... Tall, with blond hair, blue eyes, long legs, worked abs, brown skin and a trace of sand illuminated in the golden sun and a row of perfect teeth when she smiled from ear to ear! She was the happiest I had ever seen her!

Our next couple of days were filled with activities full of fun in the sun. Apart from strolling along the beautiful white sand, we went kayaking, snorkelling and took a few trips on speedboats to explore the caves and cliffs the area was known for, including 'James Bond Island'.

There are roughly two hundred islands scattered along the Krabi coastline. Some are just small rocky outcrops and many remain uninhabited. We passed where the movie *The Beach* was filmed and the evacuation zone where the earthquake and tsunami took place back in December 2004. The beaches were just out of this world, and despite being crowded with tourists, I would happily return to explore more.

My friend left three days before Christmas Eve to spend the festive season with her close family. We went for a meal just before she left. The pad thai with seafood I ordered was a big mistake, for which I paid heavily. It left me paralysed for two days straight.

The place I stayed at was tucked away in the forest and had limestone rocks that were used by climbers from all over the world, and I wanted to try it before I left, but after that lunch, and left with the strength of an ant, I could only dream about it... Big sigh!

By the time it was dark, I was alone and helpless in my room with no phone and in excruciating pain. I seriously thought I would die and never see the light of the next day again. But somehow I survived, and on day two of being confined to bed I gathered some strength and walked to reception, where a ladyboy offered me some medicine to help. He was the most sensible of them all, but they still couldn't find a spare room for me to stay. My booking was coming to an end and I had to use all of my strength to take a long-tail boat towards Ao Nang looking for somewhere to stay at the end of the day. Not an easy task in the middle of Christmas, as everything was fully booked in advance, but I managed to find a place to stay at last.

A day after that I had to do something. When I woke up it was 26th December 2015, Boxing Day in the UK. I had to make the day worthwhile after being completely useless from food poisoning and unable to do anything.

While I was in bed I did some research about what was nearby, and I found a trip off the beaten track. Himamauli would have approved of it. I booked a local taxi driver and went exploring in the mountain ranges. The hiking made me sweat, and I was still a little unsure of my health, but the trek promised a view that would take my breath away.

When I reached the mountain peak, three Christmas elves greeted me at the scene. The first elf was an enlightened lawyer from California; I haven't had the chance to interact with her as much as I would have liked. The second elf was a girl originally from the north of England with a heavy Liverpool accent that I recognised the minute she opened her mouth. She was a fun girl to be around, and she'd fallen in love on her first visit to Thailand, moved here and never looked back. She taught kids English full-time at a local school. The third elf was a Canadian man covered in tattoos from head to toe and obsessed with diving in the deep blue sea. He was in the right place to exercise his desire for this kind of thing as the nearby islands offered a huge number of diving instructor courses. Apart from that, he was pretty damn good-looking, with piercing blue eyes and a genuine smile. Little did I know that with one spontaneous act he would play a role in the story that was about to unfold. The picture he took is the front cover of this book.

After some chilling at the peak, we headed back downhill through the forest, took a swim and watched the sun go down with a Singha beer. Then a few more foreign nationals joined us at the scene. It was the best Boxing Day I could have ever imagined, better than a dream.

For the rest of my stay, there was a little crack in the ceiling of the chalet where I stayed over a couple of nights before I left Ao Nang. I thought by now that the Universe was testing my patience and was having a laugh. It's never a good sign if a woman asks for rent up front the minute you walk through her door. She couldn't have cared less about the hospitality and the comfort of her guest staying at her shack. My ceiling had a hole in it, and there were loads of cats chasing each other and fighting, jumping up and down above the bedroom where I stayed. I was horrified that the ceiling might collapse and they'd fall into my lap in the middle of the night. This didn't happen, yet each morning at the foot of my bed there was a pile of dust from the hole in the ceiling where the cats were messing about and the crack got bigger night by night. This went on for three nights in a row, each time the noise intensified, and I was waking up more exhausted than from a day in the sun heading yet for another crash at night. There was hardly any strength left in my body, yet I survived.

I discovered an energising waterfall in a national park nearby and did some yoga classes. At night I browsed restaurants with rooftop bars and tasted delicious Thai curries, washing them down with Singha beer, but I kept clear of any seafood.

Towards the end of my stay, I had a fight with my host in the backyard as I didn't have the strength to stay for a fourth night and she wouldn't return my money. Deep sigh! I hate arguments and try to avoid them at any cost... so I walked away!

The last night in Ao Nang was two nights before New Year's Eve, and with everywhere fully booked I struggled to find a room to stay overnight. Seriously, I knew the Universe was having a laugh and someone up there was testing my patience. But they don't throw rocks under your feet unless you can pull through, and I did. At last, I found a room. One moment we're up and then we're down. Life is a thin line. The secret is to walk in the middle and balance it out.

The next morning I flew back to the capital of Thailand before heading back to the UK.

***

It was my last day in Bangkok at the dawning of 2016. The aim of the day was to go with the flow, but I had one intention set in stone: to find a small temple where I could give thanks for all the blessings I'd encountered in 2015. And I did so in style, as I greeted the sunrise from the rooftop of my fancy hotel in an attempt to make my last day memorable.

Breakfast was served with a no less significant panoramic view. To enter, you had to walk through a 'Garden of Happiness', dressed appropriately. While having breakfast I looked at my current location, and the nearest point of interest was the Erawan Shrine. It was close to Siam Square, a well-known fashion district; I knew in an instant that this was my plan for the day ahead!

To reach there, I had to pass a long market street that was getting set up for another day in the heat of the day-to-day routine. A lady selling sunglasses was bang on trend, selling huge round signature 2016 'sunnies' in baby pink. I tried them on and paid straight away because they were perfect! I walked a little further and found myself in a Disney wonderland. The CentralWorld plaza was getting ready for the New Year's Eve celebration for the night ahead. I joined in the fun and felt like a character from fairyland. Little did I know that my newly acquired pink sunglasses would come in handy, and their 2016 frames would turn me into a Cinderella inside a pumpkin carriage – the perfect setting for the season's greetings from Disney wonderland!

Overwhelmed by my surroundings, I suddenly remembered the Erawan Shrine! That was the reason I'd gone there, for goodness' sake! In order to reach this holy place, I had to cross a huge intersection to get there. The shrine was in a little square surrounded by a glorious veil of glittering golden medallions that added shine to the magical atmosphere. I'd intended finding a small temple and instead found a whole experience – a traditional ritual of the Thai people in the heart of a dusty square. What I saw next was a little out of the ordinary – it was better than the Disneyland I'd left behind; the energy and the glory of this place left me transfixed by the scene. I patiently observed the local people burning incense, laying garlands of marigolds and bringing offerings to the Buddha, often kneeling down and praying for the wellbeing of their loved ones and families.

And in this humble frame of mind, an immense feeling of humility and gratitude for all life surged through my body. I marvelled at being in the right place at the right time when I set forth after walking through the Garden of Happiness in the morning and for the total feeling of bliss for being alive. And then I saw something on a marble wall, right above the square in the mall… the signature of designer Alexander McQueen was shining like a golden shield! I'd found much more than I'd bargained for; I knew he was there at the scene!

At the end of the day, I felt grateful for being human and for the feeling of deep compassion that only we can appreciate, as no other species on Planet Earth are blessed with the emotion that we carry in our hearts. It's a blessing in disguise to experience everything from happiness to extreme sorrow, regardless of faith, blood, religion, whether we were born wealthy or poor. We experience the way we feel; there is no other law.

\*\*\*

It was only later when travelling back that I found out the real story behind what I'd seen. I was extremely saddened to learn that on the 17th of August 2015, the Bangkok bombing had taken place at the Erawan Shrine and twenty people were killed and more than a hundred injured.

I had felt drawn to this destination and now understood the flow of emotions that had taken me over. I was overwhelmed by the fact that the Universe had pulled me to where this unlawful act had taken place only a few months back. I hold no respect for those who kill and carry hatred in their hearts and destroy innocent souls and create fear by spreading more fear. For those who carry love in their hearts, fear doesn't stand a chance. Despite all of the above, 2015 ended on a happy note, much as it had started. My frame of mind contributed to that, as I was on the right path towards happiness at last!

\*\*\*

I salute all those beautiful goddesses who channel their thoughts through blogs and wonderful Instagram posts from all over the world. Those who manage to sustain it, making careers out of their hobbies and travelling wherever they please. I decided to make a big trip to a far-off destination every once in a while. And I write to all those carefree female warriors out there but also to those wannabe goddesses who are afraid to step out of their comfort zone. It's the best thing that ever happened to me! Open up your horizons and liberate your souls! Freedom and love, it's all that matters! Everything else will fall into place! Just do it! Set forth the minute you step outside the airport in a foreign land, breathe in the sweet aroma of being carefree and indulge in whatever your heart desires! The world becomes your oyster and you will never ever look back!

But be warned, you ladies will become dangerous for the opposite sex. It's an endless chase! Women who become independent frighten those who are weak. For you know best, as you prove your worth, that those worth being with are hard to find as they get scared at first sight. Once you spread your wings, it takes a strong man to navigate his route alongside you. Those kings of the jungle who would take you for a ride are very rare to find!

# 19. Simply Be

As usually happens five days into the new year, it was my birthday. I'd turned thirty-three. The astrological prediction or horoscope for my zodiac revealed that this would be the year when a Capricorn would want to share. After all these years of hard work and being alone they would want to come from the surface to light and start sharing with the world. This was a promising start. Good times were on the horizon; my intention was to keep this spirit alive! Perhaps 2016 would be the best year I'd ever had! We goats are a peculiar bunch; it takes forever to build trust among other species that enter our life. To some, we may appear aloof or even stuck-up, but the truth is, behind the hard exterior we're a sensitive bunch. The people we let under our skin are selected carefully. Once we find folks that are worth our trust, we make friends for life.

There was another powerful message that came from the stars channelled by the wisdom of Kaypacha, an astrologer I started following at the time. It was rather simple but very profound: "My inner world is crowded with demons from the past, but once I know and can control them, I can master myself at last." We should heal ourselves, and once we do, we help others to heal along the way. "I want to be that light, a pure expression of love and happiness every single day of my life" – that was the thought that crossed my mind.

But the start of the year brought a challenge in my working environment that clashed with the resolution I had in mind. The amazing team we had was falling apart slightly. My beautiful team leader went on maternity leave and the new replacement started to drain my energy. I even tried dressing in white to protect my shield of light, but nothing worked against his negative energy; I was

162

absorbing his vibe. London in winter can be a dark and gloomy place, cloudy with little bright sunshine for several months. The commute to East London I had to undertake involved three hours in the underground with no natural light day in and day out. I felt like a rat. After four months, I gave up.

My next job found me, or I found them, by coincidence. I thought this might be my last stop in fashion before I left the industry behind. Truth to be told, I'd always wanted to work in a small atelier, and this place reminded of a little house with the style of a French couturier. Everything was made to measure under one roof. I was back in the borough of South Kensington and Chelsea in an established heritage company with a long-standing history. I never really wanted to have my own brand as I thought it would entirely consume my life and I'd be unable to find a balance between my work and my free time.

In the midst of it all, my romance with J No. 5 had taken me to the Austrian Alps. I'd always wanted to spend a romantic holiday up in the snow-covered mountains. This dream came true and we went off to ski for five days. I was left feeling like a spoilt princess who had it all. Being looked after and cared for by a man was something unusual in my daily life and so I had to take it all in and enjoy the ride.

Fast forward into the summer, on the 23rd of June 2016 a referendum took place about whether the UK should leave or remain in the European Union. I recall a vivid dream in the waking hours prior to finding out the truth of what was really happening in which I saw a huge spaceship plunging down into the sea. The UK voted to leave. The 24th of June 2016 in London was a very sad day. On that same morning, I was walking towards the Chinese Embassy to submit my visa application for an upcoming trip. I saw a billboard with the ripped face of former Prime Minister David Cameron. It was announced shortly afterwards that he'd resigned from his post. The future was uncertain. London was crying. You could feel it in the air, on the commute underground... everywhere. Diversity, one of the things that make this city the greatest of them all, had been shaken up. Something that was so strong had now been torn apart. My visa application to China was denied due to a lack of supporting documents. They wanted a confirmed booking of every single hotel during my trip for the entire duration of my stay, including my travel plan showing how I would reach each destination from A to B. It sounded ridiculous! I don't like rules, rules that are thrown upon us and our lives depend upon them. The 24th of June 2016 turned out to be a very sad day indeed.

Somewhere in midsummer, after this incident, Himamauli landed in the UK for a few hours before he flew back to the USA. He reminded me once again what spontaneity really is. I was invited for breakfast at the Wolseley near Green Park at the last minute, which was lovely. It was there and then that he raised a question about democracy, and whether ordinary people should actually be allowed to vote, as he referred to the outcome of Brexit. And this was before Donald Duck was voted in as the future president across the pond, about which we could raise the same point! I don't think I need to say any more!

About a month after that, I attended an Angelic Healing session with a beautiful woman in Somerset. I was invited to join her circle by one of my friends from the 'family tribe' I'd met during the Mount Shasta retreat. He advised me that the healing you receive during this session is the purest light energy he had ever encountered. I was looking forward to this special event ahead of my China trip. It took us three hours to drive down from London. Once we arrived, I met the woman running the group. She had piercing blue eyes and curly blond hair. Since I was new to her group, she asked me about the date of my birth, and this is what she had to say:

"Your life path number is the number nine – the angel assigned to your life path is Archangel Raquel and the lesson you have to learn in this life is to SIMPLY BE." I almost fell off my chair when she told me that. I couldn't believe my ears! My memories started to flick through my mind as if I'd become a supporting character in my own movie. After all the years of trying so hard to break into the fashion industry, which at times almost hurt too much, it all comes down to just 'be' and not worry about anything? Because you know you gave it your all and it still didn't work and then you start thinking perhaps there's a different path... It felt like the biggest slap in the face I'd ever had! Seriously! WOW! Simply Be at 33! Isn't that wonderful? I almost cried. Is that all there is? She made it all sound so very simple. Once again I was questioning my purpose in life. They said that once I was on my path there was no going back. The woman further revealed that she felt the energy of unconditional love and a compassionate heart emanating from my heart chakra through Archangel Shamuel, who is another guardian of mine. She had the same life path herself and was born under the same number, nine. I felt truly humbled by learning those new insights about myself. I carried out further research and discovered that people born under that number have lived through difficult childhood years and that they are very gifted human beings with lots of interests, thus it makes decision-making difficult as to which road to follow in life. It all clicked like a puzzle and made perfect sense.

We drove back to London that same evening passing Stonehenge, and I saw the world in a brand new light. I watched the most beautiful sunset from the window of the car. It all started to sink in. Acceptance for all that is, and in the simplicity of it all, I felt reborn – reborn at thirty-three! Simply be! It seems the Universe is watching me! Lyrics from my favourite Madonna album *Ray of Light* came to mind, the one where she sings that the sky fits Heaven and we should fly.

# 20. China Revelation

## PART 1. Shanghai

The China adventure turned out to be a hell of a funny ride. But I'm only saying it now as it was nothing short of frustrating at times. Although I wasn't always in the safest place, the adrenaline of not knowing what's next is the thrill in those situations! The best thing when travelling to unfamiliar places is to expect the unexpected and see what happens. Having no expectation at all is the best way to go, and with this attitude, you can't go wrong! The language barrier in the rural districts was the difficult part. But here's a fact: Oh my God, I was eternally grateful that the embassy sent me back to redo my documents! Without my thorough research in advance for the visa application the second time around, I would have been lost forever! I completely missed out on the fact that browsing the internet would be impossible once I'd arrived. Google, Facebook, Twitter or Instagram, everything was blocked by the government. Blame it on the joys of travelling to another post-communist land. Without booking in advance and printing out some maps in a country where English is limited I would have been seriously stuck. My itinerary, which had been well thought out in advance, was a blessing in disguise, and I had to stick to it like it was set in stone, because if I missed a connection I might get lost. Ohhhhh, and the Chinese love to queue and follow the rules, so I had to pretend I was lost and break their rules en route! Some of their train and bus stations were bigger than airport halls and I was overwhelmed by the scale of them. There was no point in me asking older people; they didn't understand me. Instead, I asked younger people to get clarification on which queue I should use. I was the crazy, displaced foreigner among all the ordinary Chinese folk, but if I hadn't taken a risk I might have missed a connection! There was no Plan B, only a Plan A that was followed strictly from the beginning until the end!

If you think that people in London are rude on the Tube, you haven't been in a modern cosmopolitan city like Shanghai; they'll stomp all over you! I wasn't very keen to explore the modern metropolis, but I ventured out to see the People's Square as my first stop. Believe it or not, I walked across the road and the first museum I saw was having the following exhibition: 'Iconic Shanghai – When Art Meets Hudec'. I went in, as the name carried a hint of the familiar. It was here I learned about a Slovakian architect, Ladislav Hudec, who was a First World War refugee who escaped a Russian prison camp and ran away to China to start a new life. He became one of the most respected architects in the 1930s and 1940s and helped shape the cityscape. He devoted most of his life to this city and about thirty constructions he designed have now been designated outstanding historical buildings under protection in Shanghai. I felt terribly proud, wondering what compulsion had directed me to a museum where the life of a fellow Slovakian was celebrated. My heart was beating hard so I took a long walk towards the Bund to relax. The Bund is a famous waterfront promenade celebrating the futuristic skyline of the Pudong district, a highlight destination for foreign travellers visiting Shanghai.

The following morning in the metro station at the ticket machine, I bumped into a European expat, Jean-Dominique. He explained how the system operated and we shared a few stops en route on the morning commute. During this short time, I learned that Jean-Dominique was originally from Milan and used to work in fashion for big brands, but there was no money in it, so at the age of forty-one he quit and started from scratch. Now he lived in Shanghai with his Chinese girlfriend, who was fluent in German and English and knew the European way of life, which made co-habiting easier. Jean-Dominique had lived in Poland with his former girlfriend, very close to the German border, so he also spoke the language the same as his Chinese girlfriend. He revealed that he owned a few businesses and the following morning he was flying to the city of Harbin in the Northeast of China near the border with Russia for a meeting. I wondered how old he was, as he seemed to have accomplished a lot, and he seemed pretty easy-going, which made him appear young at heart, and he had a youthful appearance on top of that. And without me saying or asking anything, he mentioned that he had a twenty-eight-year-old son! Jean-Dominique seemed like a cool guy. I asked where the funky crowd hung out and he gave me a few suggestions, and I visited this area at the end of my trip before my departure from Shanghai. European expats are thin on the ground in China. He was the first and last that crossed my path.

## PART 2. Huangshan Mountain

The next day I arrived in a tiny rural village called Tangkou, as per the plan. It was in Anhui Province under the majestic peaks of the Huangshan mountain range, the highlight of my trip. It felt like stepping back in time, and I indulged in the peace and quiet of the narrow streets around my local bed and breakfast. The friendly owner, whose name also started with a J, came to greet me, and I was pleased to hear his English wasn't bad. He kindly offered to drop me off at 6 am the following morning at the gates where I would start ascending the peaks.

My mission on day one was to start the hike from the eastern side of the mountain and follow signs to reach a viewpoint called 'Lion Peak'. It was August and it felt like the whole of the Chinese nation had decided to climb the same path that day. I was astonished to see entire families up on the hills. They took cable cars to make their lives easier. By the time I reached the base of the cable car lift on foot, they were a long way ahead of me following the same route. But I couldn't complain because the scenery was magnificent and I could concentrate on the peaks and the blue sky instead and pretend I was the only one there.

By the time I came down, it was late afternoon and I was starving. Once I reached the town, I made it straight to a local restaurant and tried to decide what to have. Chinese like their pork. I avoid eating red meat since my teenager's years and eat pork rarely. My mother always said that when I burn a lot during exercise I should eat meat as a source of protein. I ordered shredded pork with rice and ate it really quickly. After that, I strolled down to the market, watching the locals going about their daily lives and then made it back to my cosy little bed and breakfast to unwind. The place had a really good vibe, and I felt at home from the minute I arrived. But something unexpected happened that night in the safe surroundings of the bedroom where I stayed.

Before I went to sleep I lay in bed with my eyes wide open as my stomach started to feel strange. I blamed it on the pork playing havoc with my gut as I hadn't eaten any for a decade and thought I might be about to throw up. It wasn't nice. My mouth was filling up with saliva, I could hardly swallow, and just when I was about to run for the bathroom my head dropped back and I was gone...

My soul felt like it had left the cage of my body. I could see it lying on the bed motionless while I was rising above it. You might think I'm making this up, or that I'm a weirdo or a lunatic. Whatever you think, I don't give a shit! The pain in my stomach eased and I entered some kind of nirvana, or a void – a place where I wasn't physically present at all. My soul left my body and entered a very large space. I saw the stars and constellations and there were links and threads as if everything was interconnected. I didn't recognise any other souls yet I knew we were all there in a safe place. It was like being in a field of energy full of light, where everything was connected, living and breathing. But then, straight after this, I dropped down into something that felt like an underworld – a complete contrast to before. It was cold and dark and there wasn't a single living soul. The picture that comes to mind now is of the final scene in *Titanic*, where Jack and the other travellers were dead in the deep dark sea while Rose was whistling for help. That's how it felt – no breathing souls, and the empty bodies reminded me of empty shells where the souls had left them long before. They were forgotten wrecks... all frozen to death!

You can't imagine how confused I was. I'd never experienced or heard of anything like this before. I don't know how long I was gone for. All I can say is that it was a very vivid experience and perhaps I was able to look up at both sides of the Universe – a Heaven and an underworld – somewhere time didn't exist, an out-of-body experience based on real feelings.

The following day, I stood at the foot of the mountain again at 6 am. The owner of the bed and breakfast warned me that there was a strenuous route that I should avoid at all costs as not many people are fit enough to complete it. I started off ascending the western side this time, where there were fewer crowds. It was a delightful morning, with blue skies. After a while, I came to a crossing with a little bridge. Here, a few young guys ran after me to say that the next part of the route was closed, but they laughed at me and I didn't think that was nice. They shouldn't make fun of someone who doesn't know the path, and least of all tell lies... I was angry with them and carried on my way regardless.

Soon I found myself on a narrow path with steep steps, and as I climbed the second or the third flight of these, I met a young Chinese man following the same route. We embarked on this strenuous hike side by side. I climbed and then took a rest. He reached somewhere ahead of me and took a minute to pause. Then I climbed ahead of him again and stopped to catch my breath. He, in the meantime took the lead and moved ahead. After about two hours of this, we spotted a young couple coming from the other direction. I ran up to them and asked if they spoke English to see how far it was until we got to the end. The young Chinese man stood by my side; he was terribly handsome – the cutest face I'd ever seen in this foreign land. We weren't far from finishing, and after this, we started to communicate through a translation app on his phone. He wondered what I was doing there and pointed to the fact that not many people chose to embark on the hardest path and most chose the cable car. Well, I said I could ask the same question in return. He was a young man in his late twenties working in a hotel at the foot of the mountain. Today was his day off and tomorrow he would be back at work.

We reached the end and there was a fork in the road. That's

when he gave his phone to me to let me know his thoughts.

"Now the time has come for us to say goodbye and go our separate ways." It sounded so poetic that I didn't want to leave. But yes, the reality was that he was going to embark on the hike I'd done the day before, so there was no point in me doing that two days in a row. We said our goodbyes and I went to the first refreshment kiosk once I hit the touristy crowd to stock up on water and snacks. I turned around and he was there once again with that look in his eyes that said goodbye once more. After that, I never saw that cute face of his ever again. The girl in the spiritual gathering had been right when she'd said I would meet a man.

I took the cable car down to make my life a little easier this time. Back in my bed and breakfast, a Japanese couple had just checked in. I greeted the owner and told him about my victory at passing the most strenuous part of Huangshan Mountain. He told the Japanese couple that I was there on my own, and they said I was very strong for travelling alone.

## PART 3. Monkey Attack

The next morning I had to catch an early bus to Mount Jiuhua, which was a little off the beaten track. There was only one day allocated to explore there, but the bus left me further away from the destination than where I was supposed to stay. On top of that, I was in such a desperate need to pee during the journey that I shot off the minute we stopped, running into the first restaurant I saw, heading straight for the back, hoping I could find a room with a hole in the ground! And I did! What a relief! – That's when I remembered that my luggage was still in the storage space of the bus! Seriously, Andrea! – Is that what you need? To lose your belongings for a second time? Where is your head right now! The voice inside me was laughing at me! I ran from the toilet, passing the husband and wife owners of the restaurant, who were staring at me as if they'd never saw a foreigner in their entire life, and I felt bad, so I grabbed a can of Sprite and paid more than the price as I ran outside! There, in the middle of the road, my suitcase had been left behind. I took a deep sigh! The bus driver had saved me this time.

I walked back to the restaurant and asked for a taxi, but the old couple hadn't a clue what I was on about… the joys of being in a foreign land! I decided to walk down the street in this sleepy town, and after a while, I found a parking lot where there was a driver who could take me to Mount Jiuhua.

In the taxi, he spoke to me in broken English but made a remark that stood out: "You must be very religious if you are going to this town…" I wouldn't call myself as religious as he made it sound!

Mount Jiuhua covers an area of a hundred square kilometres, and within this area there are ninety-nine peaks with eighteen scenic spots and many religious shrines. It's a holy site and one of the four mountains in China dedicated to Buddhism and a well-known place of pilgrimage among the locals. The town was delightful and pleasant on the eye, and there were lovely sounds coming from the temples, a lot of which seemed to be having ceremonies taking place.

I checked into a family run bed and breakfast, possibly the only one in town, and found the owner, whose English was very limited, and we sat down. It was after lunch by the time I'd arrived and I showed him a map of a peak that I wanted to climb. But he raised a concern that people who usually climbed this route made an early start because it takes three hours to reach and I didn't have much time left to do it in the day. The problem with the Inner Child of mine is that I never listen to anyone's advice, and so I set out on the path with my map. I only had one afternoon at Mount Jiuhua and had to make the most of it.

The path was rather narrow, partially paved in concrete and partially rough ground. I wasn't completely alone; a few families with small children were also trotting along.

Suddenly the skies turned dark. Within about forty-five minutes, dark clouds completely dominated the sky and there was heavy thunder and lightning and a massive storm broke out. We were lucky, as by this time most of us on the path had reached a kind of a cliff with an overhang over our heads and we hid inside and waited for the rain to pass. Even a big scary-looking fluffy dog found shelter among us. It was another forty-five minutes until the rain ceased and everyone else started going back down. But I hadn't reached the top yet and wanted to go higher, so I carried on following the path.

According to my map, the nearest Buddhist shrine wasn't very far away, and near this temple there was also supposed to be a cable car, but I didn't know how far away it was. On top of that, there was a strange siren sound and I wondered if the cable car might be out of service because of the storm earlier.

As I continued, I reached an old woman's house. She was very cute and smiled a lot, but of course we couldn't understand each other, so I took a selfie of the two of us, and after trying to find out how far away the nearest place of interest was, I decided to go back down as it would soon start getting dark.

I walked quickly and found myself ahead of the families from the shelter underneath the cliff, and then I saw three young students teasing monkeys with empty water bottles ahead of me. A group of small monkeys appeared at the bottom of the path, and I sensed the youngsters felt slightly worried as those little monsters seemed quite vicious and possibly hungry. Live and let live, I thought to myself, and I went ahead in front of everyone to show them how it's done.

I started walking slowly, not paying attention to the monkeys, and they just passed me by. I was carrying my hands-free clutch in my right hand wrapped in a plastic bag to avoid getting my possessions wet. I walked some more, and larger monkeys started walking past and then a mother monkey with a little baby attached to her belly walked past me. I felt like a warrior, with everyone else following behind me, until, out of nowhere, this huge daddy monkey appeared below us on the path. He sat there in silence and stared directly into my eyes. I slowed down. All I needed to do was just walk past, exactly how I had with the rest of them, but as soon as I made a move towards the edge of the path, the daddy monkey moved in the opposite direction then stopped and stared again. He was looking up at me, so I tried to avoid his stare and move sideways to the other edge of the path. He did the same in the opposite direction and then stopped and stared again. After the third or fourth time of this game, I decided to go and not stop at all and avoid his glance. And this crazy daddy monkey jumped towards me, grabbed my thigh, and almost ripped my dress. As a reaction, I clutched my belongings to my chest and started screaming like mad, as loud as I could. The three boys behind me joined forces and stood up to the beast and rescued me. I called them my three musketeers. Don't ask me how. I blanked out at this point. When I opened my eyes the monster was gone and I was frightened, but not so much about being hurt, but about my bloody passport and debit card and phone in my bag that he'd been trying to reach! If all those were lost I'd be stuck in this crazy Chinese land where hardly anyone could understand me! And nobody else knew of my whereabouts! I would be fucked up big time! OK, maybe I was worried about my life too. I'm lying. I was shaking. Life *is* precious. I was terrified! The three musketeers made sure I was all right and offered to give me a lift back to the town.

## PART 4. Hongcun Village

The next morning I hit the road to explore Hongcun Village. It was the most magical place on Earth I have ever had the pleasure to discover, so full of charm and so full of mystery. It's a tiny place that was forgotten about in ancient times, and today it's a renowned UNESCO World Heritage Site, and to enter it you have to pay a fee to cross a bridge across a lake full of water lilies. It's arranged in the shape of an ox, and within its centre, tucked away deep inside hidden cobbled streets, there's a pond reflecting the traditional ancient houses adorned with red lanterns on the waterfront that add to the atmosphere of mystery.

The hotel where I stayed was possibly the only one of its kind accommodating foreigners. The interior looked immaculate, perfect as a backdrop for a movie scene or even a fashion shoot in a magazine. It had beautifully carved dark wood furniture. There was a shelving unit that had huge glass jars lined up side by side, filled with fluids and with intricate things inside. In the middle of the dining room was a heavy round table, and a big fat white cat sitting beneath it, hiding under a fuchsia tablecloth that almost reached the floor. The walls were covered with tapestries and faded paintings, Chinese calligraphy and a collage of old photographs and feathers and travellers' hats, yet everything taken together provided a kind of ambience and synergy.

My little room was right next to the dining hall, surely a place where the maid used to take a rest. It had a wooden door with a type of a metal lock that made it look more like a barn for an animal. Inside, there was a comfy bed adorned with silky pillows embroidered with golden thread. This mysterious place had a backyard with its own little pond and a garden full of wonderful plants with hidden alleyways and corners with benches. It was the most delightful courtyard, full of charm and romance. I almost wished I had someone with me.

The downside of this small gem of a village was the fact that the Chinese visit it en masse. You don't need any more than a day to explore it as it's very small. The Chinese tourists arrived in organised bus tours in the morning and left before the end of the day. I decided to spend a night there to avoid the crowd and take advantage of the silence by the lake, with its famous view of the waterfront houses at sunrise. During the day I browsed the cobbled streets and tried to see every building that was open to the public. Some of the houses dated back to the Ming and Qing dynasties. There was a beautiful house where each room inside was again adorned with ancient wood carvings and it had an opening in the ceiling so you could see the sky from the interior of every single room. Other ceilings were covered with beautiful paintings. One had a theme of children and old men with long white beards reading books in the garden under a big tree. The colours were very rich and there was writing on the wall explaining in English what it meant. The room had a scholarly atmosphere dedicated to learning and writing poetry. The painting on the ceiling was a reminder that we are *never too old to learn something new.*

These little descriptions helped me make sense of what went on all those years ago within those walls. This was possibly the first place where I actually needed some guidance, as it would have been interesting to know more about the history of these ancient buildings. The tourist groups were led by historians but it was all in freaking Chinese and none of them spoke English. Again, I was sticking out from the crowd like a sore thumb. How I wished I knew a little more about what I was looking at!

But then, outside one hall, I found this translated on the door:

Lexu Hall, also called the Hall of All Families, was built during the reign of Emperor Yongle of the Ming Dynasty in 1403, and is composed of four parts: Gateway Hall, Front Yard, Meeting Hall and Enjoyment Hall. Lexu Hall was used on occasions such as meetings, ancestry research, worship, discussion, punishment and marriage.

That was hilarious! Even in ancient times they knew that marriage was a trap when they wrote down those two words right next to each other. I guess that was the answer to wanting to know more. Freedom is the way to go!

## PART 5. Yangshuo Impressions

The next stop on my itinerary was Yangshuo in the Guangxi province. Yangshuo is best known for its dramatic landscape of the Karst mountains on the banks of the Li River. To reach this destination I had to leave Hongcun Village very early the following morning to make it back to Huangshan Bei and from there catch two bullet trains. I reached Guilin, the main city in the province, in the evening. According to my research, there was a bus that took about an hour to get to the city of Yangshuo. My rural resort was further away, hidden under a mountain peak called Moon Hill.

It was already getting dark when I reached Guilin, but I found the bus to my next destination pretty quickly. The journey itself was another surprise. The road was under construction, which made it a very bumpy ride. It took a long time, and I was tired of being on the road all day, and by now I was falling in and out of sleep, which made things a little weird.

The next time I woke up a massive thunderstorm was raging, and heavy raindrops were crashing against the windows of the bus, making it hard to see out. It was dark but there were cars everywhere, with flashing lights and beeping horns – it felt like a war zone.

After the storm, the bus stopped in a bus depot and outside it looked scary, reminiscent of a Hitchcock movie scene. I loved it! I could see mountains beyond an array of run-down hotels, with flashing red, yellow and green lights reflected in the huge wet puddles of the broken concrete floor of the depot.

I was wearing short pants and a hood over my head, and with a sleepy stare as I stepped outside the bus, I saw a handful of young teenagers running towards me asking if I needed a taxi or a motorbike. It was a sweet sight as they probably thought I was half my real age, but I could easily have been their mother. I was also dying to pee again and couldn't hold it for a minute longer.

I left my luggage with the boys and ran towards the first hotel that I saw, went straight to reception, and in desperate voice I asked for the toilet, but the man there pointed to the door! I ran back to the boys trying to explain that I needed to pee before I got a taxi, and then one of them pulled out a phone and I typed onto their mobile screen and they started laughing. One of them pointed to a dark building behind the bus depot and he went with me. I had no other choice but to follow. He stopped outside and I went inside, flashing the torch on my phone into the dark, and a strong odour hit me. I found a place with a hole in the ground and just let go. What a relief at last! Deep sigh!

Smiling from ear to ear, I headed back to my flock of hungry musketeers and showed them the address of my pre-booked bed and breakfast. One of them raised a hand, pointed to the car, and off we went into the dark. He played some underground techno as we drove through the countryside swallowed by night, and I was transported back to a clubbing scene of my youth, reminiscing about what it was like to be sweet sixteen. How I wished I could be that young once again!

My intention for this location was to slow down and cycle in the countryside to explore the stunning scenery and the hills on the enchanting banks of the Li River. And that's what I did. I made friends with the owner of the resort where I stayed. Her English was excellent. She was in her early forties, had a tiny frame and looked nothing like her real age, and she'd once lived a high-profile career in the capital, Beijing. She'd left it all behind after falling in love with the countryside when travelling down south. She and her husband made a decision to buy this property and turn it into accommodation for tourists. They had one daughter who was studying at university. I was advised which back roads to take deep into rural villages and the countryside nearby to avoid the tourists. I was armed with a map, accompanied by a two-wheeled friend and my days were filled with the joys of freedom and happiness.

I learned about a theatre play called *Impression Sanjie Liu*. It was created by the producer of the opening ceremony for the 2008 Beijing Olympic Games, and when you're in the province of Yangshuo, it shouldn't be missed. They've built the world's largest natural theatre, and it utilises the Li River as its stage with the Karst mountain peaks as the backdrop.

The performance was based on the folk tale of Sanjie Liu, who was considered the muse of the Zhuang people who lived in this region, and it's about the harmonious relationship between man and nature as he becomes an integral part of it. Hence the play gained a reputation as the 'masterpiece that cooperated with God'. It was an incredible experience, as the show used three-dimensional elements with amazing light effects reflected on the waterfront. The show takes you on an incredible journey of local Chinese tradition that involves more than six hundred beautifully dressed performers singing and dancing. This is the sort of Chinese culture that I love to watch!

The open-plan auditorium was filled with two thousand seats built in terraced rows and was sold out almost every night. I booked my ticket a day in advance to secure my spot. Believe it or not, my seat was next to a lady whose mother was from Bratislava, the capital of my country. Seriously, once again I couldn't believe what a funny coincidence I'd found myself in! Out of all the people, I sat next to a woman whose roots were Slovakian. Her father was from Israel, were she was born, and she'd never visited her mother's native land; neither did she speak the language. I discovered that she was a mother of three, whose children were grown-up and had their own families. She'd decided to sell her car and rent her flat out and then had set out on the road to travel the world with no solid plans for a year ahead. Her next destination was to embark on a journey to Japan – that country is my dream destination, and as yet it's a dream unfulfilled! At the end of the show, we made friends on Facebook and parted. She was a beautiful lady with a lovely smile and I loved her adventurous spirit!

I noticed a limestone climbing wall on day one. It was similar to one in Thailand in the Krabi islands. I knew nothing would stop me from climbing this time around!

On my last day I went for the medium-difficulty climb, although it was my first time. The instructor strapped me into the gear and off I went; the only way was up. He advised me from the bottom of the rock, telling me which direction to go in until I got stuck.

"Go to the right, lady!"

Well, I would if you told me how, little boy, I thought.

"Lady, go right," he shouted again from below.

I'm telling you I don't know what to hold on to!

"Lady, go right!"

Fuck sake, man, can't you understand there's nothing to hold on to? I didn't say it out loud. You must understand I don't use the word 'fuck', only in exceptional moments in life, like being attacked by a monkey or climbing a Karst wall mountain in freaking China! This game went on for good five to ten minutes as I was hanging there losing patience while sweating buckets of sweat out of desperation, holding on with just the tips of my fingernails! And then I started shouting back at the little boy who didn't understand: "Let me loose! I want to come down please! Let me down please!" I repeated it in case he misunderstood.

"Lady, go right," he replied.

Seriously, I can't hold myself any longer! "Down, I want to

come down! I don't speak bloody freaking Chinese! Do you understand down?" OH MAN, I'm stuck!

And since this was going nowhere, I let go, and then it hit me! I was able to move to the right after all that! You crazy lady, I thought to myself. He should have said let yourself loose and then move right. Awww, little boy, I thought to myself. If you'd explained it this way before, we could have moved on ages ago. There you go!

I pushed myself on the rope to the right, and within a minute I'd climbed up and hit the target above my head, just like that! Deep sigh of relief! Then, as I went down, turning red and purple and green from feeling hungry as I hadn't eaten and I felt sick and dizzy from being low on energy, I thought that this hell of an exercise was physically the toughest thing I had ever done... worse than paragliding in Nepal. I needed to eat something really fast!

Five minutes of resting passed by and off I went back on my bike with my head spinning. I stopped on a bridge and ate the first thing I saw – I didn't care what it was any more! Fried tofu! Greasy like hell, but never mind. I didn't throw up, luckily.

The next day, my time was up, and the plan was to travel back to Guilin in the afternoon. I was a little sad, having had a full-on adventurous time. In the morning I managed to have one more outing on my bike, but en route back, the bicycle chain gave up on me three times! Once again I was the crazy lady throwing her hands into the air stopping by every restaurant alarming all their guests having lunch trying to get my message across to get some help. The Universe was having a last laugh and I giggled inside. China must be the hardest place on Earth to get your voice heard! Luckily, I made it to Guilin on time, and the morning after, I took a cab to the airport to catch my flight back to Shanghai.

Before I left, I decided to walk one more time towards the Bund to see the famous flashing lights on the waterfront flashing into the night. Shanghai is one of those cities that never sleeps!

# 21. What's Next

Upon my return from China, a thought entered my mind. In fact, it was during the long train journey from Huangshan Bei to Guilin when I first started to play with the idea of sharing the story of my life for the first time. The frustration of not being able to talk in a foreign land had contributed to that. However, it was the out-of-body experience, something out of the ordinary, a mystery that I couldn't get my head around, and I wondered whether I should share this experience with the rest of the world.

I have wondered whether this encounter was the realisation of the scene that I painted on a piece of cardboard when I was a troubled teen, as described in Childhood Memories: the one with the thin line across a white frame divided into two halves – the upper part was full of light that represented Heaven on Earth, but it was very easy to slip down below the thin line into the darkness, or underworld. I have wondered whether the scene I painted as a child had provoked my soul to go on a journey to explore the world to try to discover the reason behind it all. My troubled self in my teenage years maybe manifested the out-of-body experience that I lived through in the Chinese mountain that my friend had foreseen in her subconscious when she said I should visit this place. Isn't that a little mysterious? Life is a peculiar journey, and we never know it all. We might not receive the answers during our time in the physical form, and that's perfectly fine as there's no beginning and no end to an evolution of a soul. Yet I was curious about the vastness of the Universe and our role in it.

\*\*\*

Once settled back in London, I made a decision to enrol onto a Kundalini Yoga Teacher Training programme. My goal was to integrate mind, body and soul into every aspect of my life and learn to emanate happiness day in and day out. It was a solid programme, with workshops taking place near King's Cross Station one weekend a month for ten months straight starting in October 2016.

During my introduction lecture to the Kundalini Yoga programme I learned that this ancient wisdom founded by Yogi Bhajan is a science that integrates the alignment between your chakra systems and the natural flow of your energetic body together with your nervous system, and thus helps to expand your human consciousness. Once you master this awareness and connect your experience with your heart, you become totally and wholly aware, and your creative potential becomes available to you.

An objective of life awakened by Kundalini is to become the best possible version of ourselves, to crystallise ourselves, to become more and more transparent and pure so we are able to project this light wherever we go.

After I signed up for the course and sat with thirty-five people in a room during the first workshop, something screamed out loud within my soul: I should do this ALONE! I was gasping for air, because following a crowd just wasn't appealing at all. I went home at the end of that day and couldn't stop thinking that something was wrong; it didn't feel right at all. I wrote a long email to the director of the course that same night saying that I needed to leave. Although I'd paid for some classes in advance, I managed to receive some of the deposit back.

In the meantime, I started playing with the idea of escaping London once more to celebrate my next birthday somewhere I'd never visited before. I didn't have time to plan a long journey and decided to visit Morocco, which would promise plenty of sun and it wasn't too far. I went ahead with this plan in search of my own light!

But before 2016 came to an end there was something else... It's one thing when someone tells you to 'Simply Be', but quite another when you leave your body. For a long time, I couldn't grasp the incident in my head and was afraid to talk to people because I thought they would think I'd gone mad. Common sense would say I'd made it all up. But as I've said before... believe it or not, the choice is yours. But the one person I could trust was W.

As the year was coming to a close, he and his partner were moving from the United States back to the UK. To my great surprise, when I mentioned to W about my experience it struck a chord with him, and he mentioned that recently he'd listened to an Australian podcast where someone else had a similar experience. I was eager to know more.

The presenters of this online podcast only scratched the surface of the topic of the vastness of the Universe but it was valuable information and it seemed that it came just at the right time, when I was questioning the 'Why?' During the episode they discussed various assumptions about how Planet Earth operates within the larger scale of the solar system, with a few references from NASA astronauts and how they perceived seeing space from orbit. One of their conclusions led to the Gaia hypothesis from the 1960s, suggesting that Earth is an ever-changing living system that is constantly evolving in the vastness of space. They made a further assumption that all living organisms, including our Planet Earth, are made of an interlocking web, and that everything is connected – as above, so below. But the strawberry on the cake during this conversation was a story by an English author Vera Stanley Alder, who described her out-of-body experience in a book called *From the Mundane to the Magnificent*.

Vera Stanley Alder was an English portrait painter and a mystic. She was regarded as someone who was way ahead of her time, investigating the realms of spirituality and self-discovery. Vera lived in London, but after the release of her first book, *The Finding of the Third Eye*, she decided to escape the city in 1939 and moved to the English countryside. It was about the same time as when the Second World War broke out. Her plan was to escape the chaos in the capital and grow a vegetable patch and work further on her spiritual quest in Essex.

After a full-on day working in the field, Vera went back to her room in the cottage where she was staying. The room was lit by silver moonlight, and she started praying like mad because up until that point she'd only ever read about spiritual matters from theory but had experienced none of it personally. She sat by her bed asking for help when suddenly a tall silhouette in a cloak appeared. He introduced himself as Raphael. Out of the blue, he called her by the name of Verity, which was her family's pet name that nobody else knew. After a brief exchange of words, Raphael asked Vera what it was that she wished to know... to which she responded that she wanted to know the Truth. She wanted to know the reason behind all the suffering on the planet and what was causing it.

Raphael explained that knowing the truth might be dangerous and that he could only teach her a fragment of the truth by showing it to her.

He then invited her to leave her body and together they conducted a series of extraordinary journeys across the etheric plane.

This is about as much as I can reveal from someone else's out-of-body experience. When I discovered the description of her first incident of leaving her physical form behind, her feeling of being nauseous and sick sounded very familiar to my own encounter in Huangshan Mountain. The rest remains a mystery. W bought me her first book, *The Finding of the Third Eye*, as a gift for Christmas that year. Her second book at the time was selling on Amazon at a retail price of £700 upwards, which was ridiculous.

Fast forward two years and her second book arrived in my letterbox; it was available at a significantly lower price. I have yet to read it, but for now I have to finish my own story. I was going to Morocco a few days before 2016 came to an end. I woke up in the middle of the night to catch a flight at exactly 3:33 am. I turned to Joanne Walmsley's numerology once again for the message that was hidden behind the number three. I found out that number three is the essence of the Trinity – mind, body and spirit. This is exactly what I aspired to integrate into my life through the Kundalini programme. It was a pleasant surprise to find out that the Universe already conspired to grant my wish. I was on the road once again to chase a new adventure, allowing the story to unfold, the last one before I turned thirty-four.

# 22. The Contrast of Existence

There is right and wrong, day and night, birth and death, and we know that one could not coexist without the other. This isn't a revelation, just a thought that entered my mind overlooking Jemaa el-Fnaa square from a rooftop bar in the bustling medina in Marrakech. Once again, I didn't know what I was looking for, but most likely it was the excitement of the unknown, as with any other destination that I hadn't been to before.

Two days earlier, I'd experienced a moment of bliss and compassion from a fellow human being following a brief period of physical pain and suffering as I caught the first rays of sunrise at the turn of a New Year, 2017, on the back of a camel in the freezing desert under the shadow of the Atlas Mountains. Thich Nhat Hanh, the Vietnamese Buddhist monk, said that once we learn to suffer, we suffer less. And I believe that to be true.

My trip to Morocco had been as spontaneous as this two-night adventure into the desert of Merzouga, booked two nights ahead of this trip. I experienced much more than I bargained for – a real adventure was about to begin, something that I wasn't aware of when signing up to the deal. One might have suspected that the temperature in the middle of a desert might be cold – even the man in the tourist agency warned me not to go. But once again I didn't listen to anyone's opinion and decided to experience it on my own. Once I set my mind upon something, there's no one in the world who can stop me from doing so.

# PART 1. Happy Crew

The trip started off in Marrakech when I stepped into a minibus with a group who would become my companions for the following three days. When I looked around, I thought it would be a boring ride, as they appeared, let's say, not very fun-looking at first glance. Perhaps the impression on the faces of my fellow passengers was based on the early morning hassle of waiting around too long before we finally hit the road.

Let me try and summarise: the seats at the very front were occupied by a young married couple from Thailand. Behind them was an Australian student with his girlfriend from Norway. They were on an internship involved with some humanitarian work with refugees – impressive stuff! Seated in front of me was a solo traveller, a Chinese guy a couple of years younger than myself, although I thought otherwise. Further down to my left were a mother and daughter from Italy spending quality time together. Three students from Korea and a gay couple from Japan were sitting towards the very back. The back seats were taken by a Turkish couple and their female native friend who lived in Canada. That was the group on the minibus, with sixteen of us, including me.

As soon as we hit the road the Chinese guy in front of me started chatting to the Australian boy across the aisle about road trips. That was something that interested me! And with my curious nature and my ears wide open, I couldn't resist joining in. Well, I don't know where it came from, blame it on the lack of sleep, and I don't even know how we got to the topic, but the first story I shared was a childhood memory of how my best friend and I killed my auntie's goat! From that point on we were in stitches laughing our heads off. The Australian boy picked up on this later, saying: "You don't start a conversation with a deadly line, especially with someone you have only just met!" LOL, I must admit he was most likely right. For the record, I didn't aim to kill this goat as some kind of revenge. My friend and I had overfed the animal, perhaps with too much grass or some sort of poisonous plant. Who knows? Either way, due to these unforeseen circumstances, the poor goat didn't see the light of the day of the following morning. The Chinese guy was hilarious too. To be precise, half of the time I had no idea what was he on about. The Australian boy and I wondered how he managed to change subjects so suddenly; nevertheless, it was very funny. I shared my impressions of the Chinese people with him, and later, after my trip, I learned a few things about the customs in his country. The Australian boy was great fun to be around, quick-witted and terribly intelligent way beyond his years. And he was obsessed with learning to write Arabic, which was admirable. Moroccan Arabic is widely spoken across the country, yet there is no standard way of writing and hardly anyone knows how to do so. Hence the confusion with roadmaps and streets that are written in different variations or have no names at all. How can a foreigner make sense of a map if even the locals don't know how to write? Just for the record, I got lost on day one when I was looking for the museum of Yves Saint Laurent. Luckily, I was saved by a local man who was very kind and didn't expect anything as a reward. We shared traditional mint tea and that was it. For the rest of the afternoon, I ended up on the back of his motorbike as he showed me around the souks that I wouldn't have entered otherwise. It takes a few days to gain confidence to enter this massive maze as you can easily get distracted by the shopkeepers… on purpose, of course, so you're tempted to buy their goods. It's more like a labyrinth, where you can get lost very easily.

Back to my newly acquired friends on the bus. We had so many laughs during the rest of the journey that my stomach hurt. And I'd thought they were the most boring bus group ever to start with! Never judge a book by its cover was the lesson learned once again!

But after laughter, there will be tears, and so there was. If I could somehow skip the following experience from the place where we stayed on the first night of our adventure I would. This was December 30th, somewhere in the valley of the High Atlas Mountains in a shabby old hotel with no heating, hot water or clean sheets. They didn't even have enough rooms to accommodate the numbers coming in, and some people were told to leave despite having paid! Complete chaos! We were treated like a herd of cattle! Reception announced we'd have to share rooms with strangers to make sure all the beds were filled and to squeeze in as many bodies as they could possibly fit in. Thinking of my feet, I proposed to the Italian mother and daughter that I could join them in a room of three. Luckily, they agreed. Deep sigh of relief! The idea of having to spend a night in a room with people I didn't know wasn't at all funny and far from ideal – especially when I was promised a bedroom to myself! I was forever grateful to my Italian companions, who felt equally betrayed. I felt the heat from the fireplace only once during dinnertime. For the rest of the night, it was beyond freezing. I was shivering all night into the sunrise, and I got up before 6 am to warm my feet by the fire before breakfast was served. After that, we hit the road in our small minibus and made a few stops to discover Berber villages en route towards the camp in the desert on New Year's Eve.

One of the places where we stopped was the Todgha Gorge. Its scenery was formed from spectacular landscapes made from a series of limestone river canyons. In the morning, the sunlight penetrated onto the walls of the magnificent gigantic rocks and lent it marvellous deep terracotta hues that were in strong contrast to the blue skies high above. It felt as if the limestone walls had an energy of their own. It felt empowering.

But before we were allowed to go outside to explore the surrounding area, a tour guide came inside the bus to explain what was ahead of us. He was a tall Berber man with a certain charm who introduced us to the nomadic way of life and show us around. At some point he mentioned there was a Japanese woman who had settled in a local village. He made me laugh with that remark, which struck a chord with my inquisitive mind, so out of the blue I exclaimed: "Has the woman fallen in love with a man or the land?" The bus crew burst into hilarious laughter!

The minute I stepped off the bus, the Berber guide put his cloak around my shoulders and announced that I should be his future wife. Now it was me who laughed, because I'm not the marrying type. We were walking side by side, with only my head poking through the cloak for a while, and I wondered how many girls he got under that same cloak throughout the course of a day... probably a few! He was tall, handsome, with incredible bone structure and high cheekbones. He was dressed fashionably and also had WhatsApp on his phone, and the next thing he asked was if I would stay with him for a while – he was persistent and wouldn't give up! When I realised he was thirty years old, I told him I didn't play games with little boys. He tried to convince me that he made his own living and didn't follow the lifestyle of his parents and that he wasn't like other guys from the village nearby who married girls young and settled down. He proclaimed that he knew how Westerners lived their lives and aspired to that lifestyle. I felt flattered that he was courteous and found me attractive; it'd been a long time since someone had paid me compliments like that. It made me giggle inside. And somehow, despite the lack of sleep and possibly being a little high from it, if anything, I was in my element, radiating warmth from and wearing my heart on my sleeve throughout the course of the day.

After introducing us to the nomadic way of life in the fields of a local village, the Berber guide took us to a traditional weaving house. It was here where I made enemies because I admired the beautiful handmade craft – the colours and patterns and shapes of those beautiful rugs – and because of my inquisitive mind I took lots of pictures on my camera, but the salesman didn't approve, because when you ask questions and want to be shown everything you like, they want to make sure you also buy. But I wasn't going to purchase anything, I simply admired the craft. They didn't know my past and I didn't know the customs of their land. I was there to invest in the experience and not to stock up on beautiful rugs!

## PART 2. The Freezing Desert

We reached the station in Merzouga for New Year's Eve ahead of when the last rays of the golden sun were descending at the edge of the Sahara desert. It was a beautiful sight. And the real adventure was just about to start...

The plan was to cross the desert on the back of the camels and join a campfire with local Berbers celebrating New Year's Eve in a traditional Moroccan style. When we arrived, we saw the last camel crew set off to the camp with the group that had arrived ahead of us. Our group arrived last and had to wait until some camels returned so we could take the same route. At first, we enjoyed ourselves in the sand, running about, jumping into the dunes, messing about and taking pictures in the vastness of the desert before the glorious veil of light disappeared. Although I was terribly tired from having had no proper sleep, there was excitement as we didn't know what lay ahead. There was a guide assigned to lead us to the camp. There were also jeeps that would take those who didn't want to wait for the camels to arrive. The Chinese guy decided to take a lift as he got bored. The Australian boy with his girlfriend and the Thai couple were led away to join a different desert camp – they must have booked with another tour guide. The rest of our group stayed together. Our guide suggested we set off across the dunes on foot as the camels we were waiting for were dropping off others in the meantime and were returning the same way. It was after seven o'clock in the evening when we set off on foot and it was starting to get a little dark.

We walked for a good half an hour and then stopped for a little break. The Korean students and Japanese guys were playing with their huge cameras and their own shadows having a laugh. I'd become close to the Italian mother and her daughter after we'd spent the night together in the hotel room, despite the language barrier. The mum spoke very little English and her daughter was only learning, but they were incredibly sweet and I knew how much the young teen was looking forward to her camel adventure. The Turkish people were sticking together, but separate from the rest of us. Apparently they'd managed to buy some booze while we were waiting at the station and were now sipping a little something along the way. The guide reassured us that the camels should be less than half an hour away from us. The sun was almost gone by now, and it was getting really dark.

Half an hour later it was pitch-black, with no sign of the camels.

We couldn't see the station where we'd come from nor any other light, just the stars above our heads and sand beneath our feet. Our guide decided to start walking again, so the rest of us followed, apart from the Turkish group who were a little behind.

A few minutes into our walk, the Turkish guy shouted from a distance: "Hey, STOP! Where are you going?"

Guide: "We are walking!"

Turkish guy: "What? I am not walking any more. You said the camels are coming so I am waiting here."

The guide moved on quickly, and we – the rest of the group – followed. The Turkish group were further behind.

"HEEEEYYY, HEEEEY!" the Turkish guy was shouting. "WAIT FOR US!"

Guide: "You said you were not going? I am not waiting!" The guide carried on and the rest of us followed. The Turkish group were chasing after us by now, and when they managed to reach us, that's when it got *interesting*!

The Turkish guy was now shouting and screaming in French at the guide. The guide got really, really angry at him, arguing about "Where the hell are the camels!"

Guide: "I don't have to go any more. I can stay right here in the middle of the desert. This is my home."

The Turkish woman living in Canada had a big mouth and she shouted back: "What do you mean you don't give a shit any more? Where are the camels? Why are we here? You said the camels are coming! Where are they?"

Guide: "I don't have to listen to this. The camels are on their way." And he stood up and started walking away from all of us again.

Now everybody was shouting at him. "HEY, WHAT ARE YOU DOING?" they screamed in despair. We all started running after him and now everyone was involved.

It was getting really interesting!

Once we caught up with him, the Italian mother started shouting at the guide in French. I wasn't quite sure what it was about, apart from the main topic of where the camels were.

The Turkish woman: "You can't just run away like that! You are responsible for all of us!"

Quite right, I thought to myself.

She carried on: "What are you doing? Why are you running away from us?"

Guide: "I DON'T CARE! GO AWAY! I CAN QUIT MY JOB RIGHT HERE, RIGHT NOW! DONT FOLLOW ME ANY MORE! GO AWAY!"

The Koreans and Japanese held themselves back and kept quiet, as you would expect. I had a question that I didn't bother to ask at this point as I wouldn't get a word in anyway.

The Italian mother started asking him about calling someone to find out how long the camels would take. She asked him to inform someone about our location and to send camels to meet us. At that moment we realised his mobile phone was dead.

"WHAT?" People were shouting. "NOBODY KNOWS WHERE WE ARE!"

That was no longer *interesting* – it was *totally amusing*! We wondered if anybody actually knew where we were. You couldn't see anything apart from the stars and sand for miles on end. From time to time we heard jeeps in the far-off distance, but not close enough for us to fetch one.

Now they were trying to find out if someone had a portable charger for the guide's phone so we could get hold of someone. After a couple of minutes they worked something out and the guide was trying to call people from the agency we'd booked the trip with. But of course, nobody was picking up. Not at this hour of night. This performance went on for a good hour or two – with *no* outcome, *no* camels, *no* jeep… just the stars above our heads and the sand beneath our feet.

The people were becoming increasingly frustrated and aggressive.

The loud Turkish woman confided in me that she was getting really frightened of being lost. I don't think you can get lost in the desert, I thought. I was much more concerned about the freezing cold. All I wanted to know was how far we would have to walk if we were to reach the campfire by foot, or whether it was a shorter distance to walk back to the station where we'd come from... and so I went to ask the guide.

ME: "I have only one question, please... only one question."

He was sitting in the sand, cross-legged, with anger on his face at this point, and he hardly looked up at me. In fact, he didn't look up at me. He didn't say anything. I wasn't going to get a word from this man. Nothing at all. I was fairly amused by the whole situation. If I hadn't been getting cold and exhausted from the lack of sleep I would have laughed about the whole thing. I was wondering how far we'd actually walked from the station, as it didn't feel like we'd walked too much. But then you couldn't see any lights in any direction, just the stars above and the sand below. It was pointless to guesstimate. We only had to believe that the camels were still coming as the guide had promised. But in my opinion it was terribly irresponsible of him to claim that he didn't care... or that he could leave his job right then. Obviously someone must have put him in charge to be our guide!

The others were still trying to call someone to let them know where we were. People didn't care if they called camels or jeeps! Although I knew that the Italian girl would have been terribly disappointed if the camels didn't arrive. She'd been looking forward to this adventure for the entire trip. We would have a terribly disappointed and broken-hearted teenager if jeeps were to take us there instead. I still had some battery left on my phone, although there wasn't a signal, so there wasn't any point. We'd heard the engines of cars and jeeps in the far-off distance. And the quiet Asians and I started jumping up and down screaming our lungs out and flashing our phones in the air. We shouted loudly for HELP into the dark.

"HEYYYYYYY... HEYYYYYYY... HEYYYYYYY! WE ARE HERE! HELP!"

But nothing. They didn't see us. After that, we heard another car in the distance and we shouted our hearts out all over again.

"HELP!"

Jumping up and down as high as we could with our phones in

194

the air.

"HELP!"

They were coming towards us at last! YAY! Finally! They'd seen us! We were jumping up and down with a deep sigh of a relief thinking we were safe. But when the car turned up it was full. The guy behind the steering wheel looked at us and asked which tour operator we were with. He couldn't help us at all. He just drove off.

Our attention went back to the guide who couldn't give a shit. I bet he didn't care if the camels were coming or not by this point. We were stuck there – all on board the same boat. People were yelling and shouting at him until he got up and started walking away from us again. Oh *man*, he walked fast. We started running after him as he was the only one who knew where we were. He was the only one at home in the vastness of the desert.

The Turkish people screamed at him again: "WHERE ARE YOU GOING? YOU CAN'T LEAVE US ALONE!"

Here we go again, I thought to myself.

The guide screamed back: "IT'S ALL YOUR FAULT! IF YOU HADN'T GONE TO BUY ALCOHOL, WE COULD HAVE GOT ON CAMELS AGES AGO!"

The Turkish gang in response to that: "WHAT THE HELL! THAT'S NONE OF YOUR FUCKING BUSINESS! WAIT!"

Wow! It went from *interesting* to *really interesting* to no longer interesting but *totally amusing* and then HE NAILED IT! That statement wasn't supposed to be said out loud! OH MY... I don't use the 'F' word unless I have to. Trust me, it's not very ladylike. But I had no other choice. Fucks and other F'ed-up words were flying in the effed-up air like a bunch of drones! Oh man, the guide had no right to judge. It was New Year's Eve, for F-sake, and the Turks were on their holidays! That was a really inappropriate remark from the guide. Sometimes it's better to bite your tongue.

A thought crossed my mind: the guide was jealous because they had booze and he didn't, not a single drop. Instead, he added more fuel to the fire of a fierce Turkish mind. A fight was on, big time, until someone shouted out: "CAMELS! Camels are coming!"

Camels started appearing from the darkness. AT LAST! I think I would have felt better in a jeep, but there wasn't one.

It took us about an hour to reach the tent with the campfire at last. But the stars! Oh my goodness the stars! They were fucking awesome and magical! And I was fucking frozen from the freezing desert and the precious Universe above my head to the core of my freaking bones!

And that was only the start. Once we'd reached the campfire the Chinese guy lifted me up in the air as he said: "Where have you been so long?"

"Well, best not to ask," was my advice.

It felt like an eternity since he'd got the lift in that car, and I wished I'd done that.

Our group sat down in a tent around a huge round wooden table. They were serving an enormous wooden dish of chicken tagine, a traditional Moroccan meal with bread, which we all shared. At last, something HOT! Hmmmmm, it felt so good! The best thing so far! Although anything hot would have eased my hunger after the never-ending camel ride. All the other tourists must have had their dinner already served, and we were the last. There were about eighty of us from tour operators and then locals started to join us. Outside the tent, crowds were gathering around the fire playing traditional Moroccan drums and chanting. Even though I love fire, I only stayed for a little while. The fire was actually much smaller than I thought it would be and I wasn't in such a great mood for celebrating outside with the stars. My happiness faded as quickly as the temperature dropped. It was minus five degrees Celsius. My main concern was where I would lay my head down for the night, or if I'd get any sleep at all. Apart from the main tent, there were a few smaller ones where people could take a rest. I overheard someone saying that each tent had space for about six people – and this was going to be a difficult task. I wanted to stay with my group, which now consisted of eight people, excluding the Turkish gang, as they preferred to lay their heads down in the main tent instead. So we all squeezed in, or rather I squeezed in, as everyone else had found their spot when I joined them. Imagine the tent: eight people lying horizontally, one next to another, with backpacks in the corners. I had to dig out a spot to myself between everyone's stuff, vertically alongside people's feet. Basically, there was no other room available. And there was no heating. My feet were touching the curtain of the entrance of the tent, so anyone that walked in or out let in a blast of ice-fresh air. That wasn't funny at all! I'm telling you... I was suffering, big time! I lay there with only a blanket beneath my body. The tent was made with a layer of plastic covering the ground and I had one other blanket to cover myself with. I didn't have a proper jacket, only a thermal long-sleeved top, jumper and a vest. Luckily, I did have a hat, scarf, gloves and trainers on my feet, although my toes were already totally numb.

It was about midnight when I tried to lie down – the longest New Year's Eve I had ever experienced in my entire life! Of course, I didn't get any sleep. My feet were frozen and I lay there listening to the noise of the other people from the camp while massaging my toes. There were all sorts of noises outside. Then, I needed a pee. I held it for a good two hours as I couldn't be bothered to get up to empty my bladder. But then I had to, badly. It was 3 am when I ventured out into the desert to find a quiet spot where nobody would see. Well, that was a hard task, as many people were still out and about flashing lights all around the camp. I made my way behind the tents and didn't use the torch on my phone on purpose, so nobody would see me. By this time I was laughing at myself and about the situation I was in, trying to find a spot in the sand in the middle of the Sahara desert. Finally, when I thought I was safely away from the rest, I flashed the light on my phone to see where I was. Ooooopss! I almost stepped on a camel's head! LOL, this was getting better and better by the minute. As long as I can laugh about it, all is good!

Relieved, I went back to my spot in the tent. It felt like another lifetime until I got up again, counting every hour–minute–second– nanosecond into the sunrise... So much for being present and mindful of the situation I was in. It felt like an eternity. I repeated to myself the wise words of my spiritual guru Osho about suffering: "This too will pass". And it did. Finally, the sunrise arrived at last.

I jumped out of the tent, as I couldn't wait any longer for the other people to wake up. The Italian girl could sleep anywhere, no matter what. I envy those people a lot. Outside, it was chaos again. I walked around asking random people what was going on. I wanted to know if there was any organisation in place to arrange travel back. And they were giving me looks as if: "Who the hell are you and why do you ask?" I was desperate to know how quickly we could go back to the station where we'd come from the night before.

After running around like a headless chicken I realised there was no point in that. Was I surprised? NO! I was hoping to get a lift back in a jeep, but I couldn't see any. And then I spotted the Italian mother and daughter running towards the camels in the distance. Not again!

I ran after them, asking if they wanted to get a car instead. I almost begged them to wait with me for a jeep, but the girl almost broke down in tears as she was desperate to get on a camel's back once again. At that moment I realised I was better joining them before the supply of camels was short again. Was I ready to survive another slow-motion journey on the back of those animals in the freezing temperatures across the Saharan desert? I wasn't terribly convinced!

On the 1st January 2017, my Italian companions and I climbed onto the back of the camels among the other travellers and set off on a slow journey across the dunes, watching the sunrise greet the New Year. I wrapped my legs tightly across the camel's back and kept massaging my limbs en route to keep my blood circulation running. As we were moving at the speed of a snail, I found that I couldn't feel my limbs. Towards the end, my torso swung back and forth to the natural rhythm of the animal's body movements, and I could hardly feel anything. The freezing cold was digging deeper into every single living cell of my body. Suddenly, I saw the trees. They were still quite far away, but they were the trees that I'd seen by the station where we set off the day before. But then the trees disappeared. Hmmmm, was I hallucinating, or what? Or perhaps we were passing a deep dune so I'd lost them from view. I started to feel nauseous and sick in my stomach towards the very end. The trees reappeared! Thank God, I wasn't hallucinating! The end was here! Finally!

The camel lowered itself according to the guide's instructions and I stepped down. I literally broke down. My knees dropped into the sand and I fell flat on all fours and my body collapsed. There was slight amusement that rang in my ears from my fellow passengers behind, but it stopped as soon as I burst into tears and wept. I couldn't help myself. I wept because I couldn't move. I wept because my strength had left my body and I couldn't feel my limbs. My Italian companions raised me up and gave me support as we headed towards the station where breakfast was being served. I took off my trainers and poured hot water over my feet. Nothing – I couldn't feel a single thing. My toes were dead. I repeated the process, dipping my hands into the water as well. After a while, those started to feel alive again, but my toes were still totally numb. I put my trainers back on and jumped up in the air to see if I could feel anything. I couldn't. I repeated this process for about fifteen to twenty minutes, jumping up and down like a lunatic. We had Moroccan bread with jam and mint tea for breakfast. I felt like Jesus Christ who rose from the dead when I started to feel my senses coming back.

As I sat there, my eyes met the gaze of the Italian mother and we burst into hysterical laughter. I will never forget the sparkle in her eye. I was speechless, but the expression in her eyes spoke a thousand words – it was all that was needed. In that simple gesture, a connection was made, a connection of a fellow human being's compassionate heart that bonded with mine. The bliss of this encounter wouldn't have emerged without me throwing myself into the unknown in the first place.

The thought in my head when I first collapsed into the desert was: why the hell do I need to punish myself this way? Have I not done enough shit of this kind in my younger years? In a few days, I would reach thirty-four. Was I scared of getting old? Did I really need to put myself through these pilgrimages? I believe I was hungry once again for adventure and the adrenaline that comes with the thrill of the unexpected. Maybe I was looking to embrace the authentic experience under the vastness of the sky with the stars above my head and the sand beneath my feet. Perhaps I was craving the warm human touch or the act of kindness of a fellow man that I was missing as a little child. Who knows? We don't need to have answers for it all, as I've said before.

When I walked outside the station I found the guide from the previous night sitting on the steps in front of the entrance, and this time he looked up at me and said: "Can I tell you something?"

I nodded. …

He said: "You are a good person."

Wow! The funny thing was, it had cost me frozen limbs and a dark night lost in the desert to get an answer from this Berber guide. He made me laugh, big time. In the meantime, someone mentioned that it had been his birthday last night. I was right when I thought he was jealous because he didn't have a single drop of drink. No wonder he wanted to quit his job and celebrate instead. He was a stubborn Capricorn goat, just like me, who couldn't give a damn! What an experience! OH MAN! Well, that would certainly be a new year to remember. Here's to embracing pain, to happy memories, or rather the alchemy of happiness through suffering. At the end of the day, it's the experience that makes any trip worthwhile.

## PART 3. Drawing with Light

Towards the end of my stay in Marrakech, I paid a visit to the Photography Museum hidden in the narrow streets of the Medina labyrinth. The collection contains hundreds of old photographs capturing scenes of everyday life, as well as an archive of images from the history of Morocco. Here is a short introduction to the collection that I read on the wall:

The variety of the landscape, the hospitality of the population, and the light: these are the characteristics of Morocco. The collection of the museum aims to show the passion that Morocco excites, and to highlight a heritage and history, which stands alongside the great treasures of humanity. The exhibition, 'Morocco, Land of Light', has selected original photographs taken by both European and Moroccan photographers. In Arabic, the word 'Photography' translates as 'To Draw with Light' – What better translation could be there for these fragile photographic documents?

As I stood there in awe of what I'd just read, I received a reassurance that I should tell the story of my life, to leave my own trace of light behind. At the end of the day I'd been brought here to realise, aged thirty-three, that I only need to 'Simply Be'. It seems the Universe is already watching me.

As I walked back to reach my small traditional Moroccan riad, I had to cross a long street full of market stalls. I walked pass this narrow street a number of times each day to avoid the shopkeepers. When I was passing this time, something struck me. I had previously lived this experience in one of my dreams! In this dream, I ran through a narrow street just like the one in this scene! But in the dream I was being chased by something, only I didn't know what it was. I woke up sweating a number of times in the middle of the night wondering what was chasing me. All I knew was that I was running desperately. And then it *hit me*. I was running in foreign lands, chasing my own light. I was searching for the one who had already arrived. I was running through the streets of Marrakech to realise that the one who I'd chased all this time was myself! Because by now even I had forgotten about the quest I'd set my life upon in the Himalayan mountain range. All this time I'd been on a quest to find the voice behind the mind sitting on the windowsill in Nepal with a question and a tear in my eye, wanting to know who I was.

Who am I? The child that felt it didn't belong to its roots. The hungry teenager wanting to learn and grow with no future in her native land that had to be left behind. The lost adolescent finding her feet in a foreign country while learning to speak a new language so her voice could be heard. The student who had to prove her ambition in her desired career, thinking fashion was her true path. The adventurer that lost her belongings in Bali, only to realise that material things mean nothing at all. A further escape took place in my search for happiness and to relieve the pain of separation from my own family. A return to innocence – a return to my own truth, following the realisation that all I need to do in this journey called life is to 'Simply Be'! And then to fall flat on my back and leave my body behind and wonder what it was all about? The contrast between existence and transcendence beyond the realms of the conventional mind. And then I was back on the road again! This time I chased my own freedom through suffering in the freezing desert under the vast sky and running after my own light in the streets of Marrakech only to realise I had already found myself! The truth is that I am everything – I am all of the above and nothing at all! Just the pure energy of love and light connected to the source. The truth is that we are the life in this Universe and the Universe is in all of us!

Today I know better. Today I know that the feeling of not belonging as a child was only an illusion created in my own mind. Ironically, members of my own family contributed towards this feeling that I had to unlearn through the enlightenment that was experienced on Huangshan Mountain. It was here that I discovered that we are all interconnected under the vastness of the sky. Imagine children who will put aside the fears and anxieties that their parents lived with, or inherited from the karmic wheel of their families, and those children giving birth to a new generation of kids being free of their parents' fears. Imagine generation upon generation freeing their souls step by step, little by little, living life closer to the pure energy of love and light that we were all created with.

Imagine happiness is your birthright and living in the present moment to serve your highest good is your only obligation in this life. Each and every single one of us carries their truth locked inside their heart. And a compassionate heart eliminates fear; these are the true lessons we came here to learn in our lives.

There is only one universal truth, with one law of attraction towards its core. To simply become one with it all, one has to eliminate fear and walk a path towards enlightenment to find unconditional love, because only with open hearts we will be at peace and experience the ultimate freedom, joy and happiness that we all seek. That simple state of knowing nothing and no one is separate, and we are all interconnected to the source and the source is one and so is the truth. We are the children of the Universe and Mother Earth gave life to us all. Let's protect, celebrate and be grateful for walking her soil!

\*\*\*

Towards the end of the trip, on my birthday, when I turned thirty-four, I treated myself to a spa with a traditional Moroccan hammam experience. I felt like a little girl who had been scrubbed to the core of my being with the spices and natural fragrances from the soil of the Earth. The experience of having my naked body washed by affectionate hands of the divine force of a mother's sensible touch left me feeling pampered beyond words. After that, my skin was revitalised with oil and a full body massage. It was pure heaven, bliss and enlightenment all at once! I was reborn all over again!

Perhaps my trip to Marrakech contained the last pieces of my storyline to convince me that I'm on the right path to start writing my own story down. After visiting the Photography Museum and reading the sentence about drawing with light, it felt as if the Universe had sent me the last signal for going ahead. And everything felt in alignment with my life purpose and the reason for being in the right place at the right time. Perhaps this story was the piece of work I ought to create all along. It didn't hit me until I read my old diaries and saw a journey with a story unfolding. My life up to the age of thirty-three had come full circle, and my second birth was yet to begin.

I came to realise I was the beacon of my own light from chapter 1 when I met the psychic man that gave me the key to step out on my own spiritual path...

I found the following words on the Divine Love Frequency's Instagram feed and I decided to share them here. They brought tears to my eyes whenever I needed the strength to tune into my writing, for they are among the most divine words I have ever come across from another soul:

You know your power. And you must also know that this power is the power of all of humanity. Your power is choice, choosing at will the divine love frequency that expands your being. So what will you do with this power? The only thing you can and must do is to fill yourself with love, and move this love into the world you live and love in. Wake others up with your love, for your love is also their love, and with this may you empower. (Marinone, 2017)

Some people say that I live in a fairyland. I must be a fool to reveal my soul. It takes courage to be stupid enough to reveal it all. A certain amount of naivety and innocence has been kept. There was a time I learned to unlearn all that I'd ever learned. All they imposed on me was dropped and I was shaped to believe only that which I felt. The truth became the experience I lived in my own skin. After all the cruelty and sadness in this world, I choose to wear glasses in a shade of pink.

Because I choose to believe in the human race.
Because deep down we all crave to be accepted for who we are.
Because love is unconditional and the power of love is boundless and eternal.
Because love is light that transcends all hatred and hate.
Because we live in a physical form for only one lifetime and that time is short.
Because the love I carry within my being melts all darkness away.
Because I want to be happy for as long as I live...

And for this reason I choose to believe in magic and look for truth over and over again, wearing my heart on my sleeve!

# Bibliography

Alder, V. S., *From the Mundane to the Magnificent* (London: Rider, 1988).

Bach, R., *Jonathan Livingstone Seagull* (London: Harper Element, 2003).

Bach, R., *The Bridge Across Forever* (London: Pan Books, 1984).

Bhajan, Y., Lecture: What is Yoga? Part 1, Retrieved from

https://www.3ho.org/kundalini-yoga/yogi-bhajan-lecture-what-yoga-part-1, dated November 6, 2017.

Coelho, P., *The Alchemist* (London: Harper Collins, 2006).

De Saint-Exupéry, A., *The Little Prince* (England: Wordsworth Editions, 1995).

Dream Moods, *'The interpretation of a lion and a mouse'*, Retrieved from

http://www.dreammoods.com/dreamthemes/animals2.htm, dated March 13, 2017.

Marinone, A., 'Divine Love Frequency' [Instagram post], Retrieved from https://www.instagram.com/p/BSmCz7Qgxej/, dated April 7, 2017.

Osho, *Courage, The Joy of Living Dangerously* (New York: St Martin's Griffin, 1999).

Osho, *Love, Freedom, Aloneness* (New York: St Martin's Griffin, 2003).

Osho, *The Book of Secrets* (New York: St Martin's Griffin, 1998).

Walmsley, J., *'Angel Numbers Joanne Sacred Scribes'*, Retrieved from

http://sacredscribesangelnumbers.blogspot.com/2015/08/angel-number-2222.html, Feb 12, 2017.

Walmsley, J., *'Angel Numbers Joanne Sacred Scribes'*, Retrieved from

http://sacredscribesangelnumbers.blogspot.com/2011/08/angel-number-333.html, Oct 15, 2017.

Weiss, Dr B., *Many Lives, Many Masters* (London: Piatkus Books, 2007).

Printed in Poland
by Amazon Fulfillment
Poland Sp. z o.o., Wrocław